THE 12 SECRETS OF PERSUASIVE ARGUMENT

THE 12 SECRETS OF PERSUASIVE ARGUMENT

Ronald Waicukauski, Paul Mark Sandler, and JoAnne Epps

AMERICAN BAR ASSOCIATION
Defending Liberty
Pursuing Justice

on the ability to communicate persuasively. In this book, three masters of their craft share their stories, strategies, and suggestions.

The authors offer practical tips about how to deploy the 12 basic techniques of forming and delivering persuasive arguments. Along the way, they also will amuse and provoke you with real stories from their practice and the lessons we should learn from them.

As lawyers, we constantly strive to improve our skills. I know this book will help you become a more persuasive advocate, and I hope it will entertain you, too!

Carolyn B. Lamm
President, American Bar Association

Contents

Introduction

Argument is the fundamental tool of the lawyer's craft. As lawyers, we argue to persuade juries to render favorable verdicts, to convince judges to grant motions, and to induce appellate courts to correct errors. In less formal settings, we argue to persuade witnesses to cooperate, to convince opposing parties to settle, and to achieve myriad other objectives, large and small.

We are professional arguers. Clients employ us to argue on their behalf, to be their advocates. Notwithstanding this paramount role of argument in our work, few of us have given much attention to argument as a subject of study. In learning to think like a lawyer during law school, most of us developed a sense for recognizing a sound legal argument. There is, however, much more to the process of crafting a persuasive argument than possession of the analytical tools learned in law school.

Many factors contribute to the persuasiveness of an argument. Because these factors are critical to our work as lawyers, they need to be recognized and understood. We need to be able to employ them quickly and effectively whenever we argue. Each of the twelve secrets described in this book concerns a material factor that influences the persuasive effect of any argument.

These twelve secrets of persuasive argument did not originate with the co-authors. In fact, some of these secrets were first identified more than 2,000 years ago in Aristotle's *Rhetoric*, the most influential book ever written on the subject of persuasive argument. Other secrets were initially explained in the classical writings of Quintilian, Cicero, and Demosthenes. Still others are derived from the work of contemporary scholars in communications and social psychology, and others are distilled from the authors' own collective experience of more than 100 years as trial lawyers and teachers of trial advocacy, as well as from the experiences of some of the greatest lawyers of all time: Daniel Webster, Abraham Lincoln, Clarence Darrow, Edward Carson, Charles Russell, Rufus Choate, and more.

Our discussion here focuses on arguments presented orally by lawyers to persuade judges, jurors, arbitrators, mediators, and others in structured legal settings. Nevertheless, it should be understood that these concepts apply to arguments in virtually any context, whether formal or informal, legal or nonlegal, written or oral.

We do not pretend to know how to argue and win every time. What we do know, based on ideas from some of the world's greatest thinkers and advocates, is how to make the most persuasive argument available and thereby maximize the likelihood of success.

Secret 1 Focus on Your Goal

The usual purpose of a lawyer's argument is to persuade a decision-maker to decide in the client's favor. This desired action is the goal that should guide the preparation and presentation of your argument. It was said that when people heard the Greek orator Demosthenes, they often remarked, "My, what a pretty speech"; but after hearing Cicero, they shouted, "Let us march!" As a lawyer, your goal is to make the argument that not merely impresses but, like Cicero's, induces the desired action. Everything that you say or do in making an argument should be determined on the basis of whether it will help to induce the desired outcome.

Identify Your Primary Goal

Clarify your goal. Before preparing an argument, whatever the context, you should first determine precisely what it is you hope to achieve. As Casey Stengel warned, "If you don't know where you're going, you might end up someplace else." Sometimes your goal will be obvious—e.g., to win a defense verdict for your client. Often, it may not be this clear. Think about your goal carefully. Then, describe it in one crystal-clear sentence so you know exactly where you are heading.

Choose a realistic goal. As James Russell Lowell explained, "There is no good arguing with the inevitable. The only argument available with an east wind is to put on your overcoat."[1] Circumstances sometimes dictate that your sights be set on a lesser target than the total victory your client may demand. In defending a civil case in which a defense verdict appears impossible, for example, your goal might be to limit damages and your argument directed accordingly.

Identify Secondary Goals

In some cases, you may identify multiple goals. In a summary judgment argument, you may seek to win the motion but, if that fails, to persuade the judge and opposing counsel that the case has less settlement value than they think. Winning the motion may be the primary goal and the secondary goal to posture the case for a favorable settlement.

Identify Intermediate Goals

Determine the underlying claims. There may be intermediate goals that, if achieved, will facilitate realization of the ultimate goal. To understand the intermediate goals of an argument, consider the concept of "claim." In this context, "claim" refers to a proposition that you, as an advocate, seek to have accepted by your listener.[2] In a routine personal injury case, much of your argument for the plaintiff would be concerned with the reasons, supported by the law and evidence, that the plaintiff's claim of negligence should be accepted. The jury's acceptance of this claim is an intermediate goal of your argument. The ultimate goal of your argument, of course, is the award of a substantial plaintiff's verdict. In your typical argument, there may be several claims that provide the logical building blocks that lead your listener to the desired outcome. In the example of the personal injury case, these claims might be that the defendant was negligent by driving drunk; the defendant's negligence caused the plaintiff's back injury; and the back injury prevented the plaintiff from returning to work for two years. The jury's acceptance of each of these claims is the intermediate goal of your argument.

Identify other supporting objectives. Other goals include Clarence Darrow's belief that "the main work of a trial attorney is to make a jury like his client," or inducing the jurors to identify with you—to believe you are similar to them and, therefore, a person whom they can trust. If the jury identifies with you and likes your client, the probability of a favorable verdict is materially enhanced. [*See* Secret 3, Cultivate Ethos.]

Use Your Goals to Direct Preparation of Your Argument

When preparing an argument, keep your ultimate goal clearly in mind. As you think through your case, continually test any point you might make by asking, "How will this help to achieve my goal?" In golf, every stroke you take should advance your ball toward the hole. In argument, every point you make also should advance your goal. For example, if you represent a plaintiff opposing a summary judgment motion, your ultimate goal is the court's denial of defendant's motion. An intermediate goal might be acceptance of your claim that there are genuine issues of material fact. While preparing your argument, you consider arguing that the evidence in favor of the plaintiff is so strong that a plaintiff's verdict at trial is overwhelmingly likely. Does the point help you achieve your goal? For purposes of the motion, you want the court to focus on the narrow question of whether there is a genuine issue of material fact. Making the point about the strength of the evidence raises the bar you must jump to survive the motion. The task at this stage is not to evaluate the overall merits of the case, so it does not help you to suggest that it is. Stay focused on your goal and reject the idea of making that particular point.

Follow a Brief Outline to Stay on Course

Stay focused. During an argument, temptations may arise that can distract you from your goal. Opposing counsel may make irrelevant points that you want to decimate. Clever comments may come to mind. Beware of such temptations. Use a short outline of your main points to help you stay on course. Think of your outline as a map to guide you to your desired destination. There may be appropriate times for a detour, but be cautious, lest you lose your way.

Allow for spontaneity. Do not become so wedded to the outline that you forsake all spontaneity. Avoid reading your argument, because you will lose eye contact with your audience and limit your ability to observe and respond to your listener's reactions. Instead, follow the example of Archibald Cox, one of the greatest appellate advocates of all time. Even in argument before the U.S. Supreme Court, he reduced his argument to notes on a single sheet of paper.

Establish an effective framework. As you prepare your brief outline, consider this classic scheme for presenting your argument: begin with what you are going to tell the jurors; tell them; and conclude by telling them what you told them. This framework will help you maintain your focus on the precise points that, after careful reflection, you selected as the most useful in achieving your goal. [For guidance on organizing your argument, *see* Secret 8, Strategically Arrange Your Arguments.]

Use Moot Court Sessions to Prepare

Practice responding to questions. When arguing before judges, you will often be required to answer questions. Such questions should be welcomed because they can provide important information about what a judge is thinking and give you an opportunity to respond directly. Nevertheless, questions can also make it more difficult to stay focused on your goal. Rehearsing your argument in a moot court format can help. Practice with an audience that interrupts you with questions—these could very well reflect the types of questions that will be in the minds of your listeners when you actually present the case.

Thurgood Marshall reportedly mooted his famous *Brown v. Board of Education* argument at Howard University Law School the day before he was scheduled to appear in the Supreme Court. During the practice session, a student serving as a moot court justice asked a question that stumped Marshall. Marshall spent the evening thinking about the question and developing a strong response. As it happened, the same question was posed by one of the Supreme Court justices the next day. Marshall's preparation contributed significantly to the achievement of his goal of obtaining a landmark decision in favor of desegregation.

Develop transitions to your main points. As you work on developing good answers to questions, consider how you might transition from those answers to the main points you want to emphasize. In using a moot court session, practice weaving the points you wish to convey into your answers. Suppose, for example, you want to argue that the plaintiff lacked standing but, before you reach the point, the court asks, "Counsel, did the trial court have jurisdiction to hear the case?" You answer, "Yes, Your Honor, the Court did have jurisdiction to hear the case, but we contend that the plaintiff lacked standing to bring the case." If you are arguing before a court that asks frequent questions, you will soon realize that you may not have enough time to present all of your argument unless you have developed the skill of transitioning from your answers to your main points.

Concede weak points that could cloud strong points. One example of an appropriate concession occurred during a claim against a bank for wrongfully invading a customer's account to pay the negative balance on the account of a related business. The bank's defense was that the owner of the related business account had authorized the transfer of funds. Plaintiff's counsel conceded that the owner had authority to instruct the bank to transfer funds but argued that the owner had not exercised the authority. That the owner had authority was a good point to concede, because the bank could have produced written documents proving such authority, and a battle over interpretation of the documents would have clouded the issue whether authority actually had been exercised. By avoiding a battle over a weak point, plaintiff's counsel focused the jury's attention on an issue that was much stronger for his client.

Identify What You Can and Cannot Concede

A moot court can be helpful to determine what you can concede that will be consistent with reaching your goal and what you cannot concede without sacrificing your goal. Zealous argument does not require, or even suggest, that you resist all concessions. In fact, knowing when to concede a point is a mark of effective advocacy. When you properly concede a point, you keep the focus on the important facts or law of your case. You enhance your ethos because admitting the unfavorable point serves to demonstrate that you are being truthful and fair. [*See* Secret 3, Cultivate Ethos.] Making the appropriate concessions can actually strengthen the points you want to emphasize. Be careful, however, not to concede too much. Before presenting your argument, locate the line behind which you cannot retreat without jeopardizing your goal.

Resist the Temptation to Play to the Gallery

Remember that the decision-maker is your key audience. When you are engaged in argument, it is alarmingly easy to lose sight of your goal. One reason for this is that in addition to being an opportunity to persuade a judge or jury, an argument is also an opportunity to impress the gallery. In televised trials, there is even the temptation to play to the television audience. Resist such temptations because they divert you from your real mission—persuading the decision-maker.

Avoid negative effects on the decision-maker. Not long ago in a court trial in Nottingham, England, counsel succumbed to the temptation to play to the gallery during his final argument. Earlier in the trial, a tape recording had been introduced into evidence and, rather than consume court time, the judge, at counsel's suggestion, decided to listen to the tape on his own time. Later, counsel inquired whether the judge had listened to the tape. The judge replied, "I did but dozed off. Then I replayed the tape and listened to it all." During closing argument, counsel argued that since the judge had fallen asleep, he had not listened carefully to the tape. The judge interrupted, reminding counsel that, after "drifting off," he had rewound the tape and listened to it all. The judge then abruptly terminated counsel's argument, saying he had heard enough, and ruled for the other side. Counsel's point about the judge's sleeping may have played well in the gallery. The judge, on the other hand, was not amused. If counsel had stayed focused on his goal of persuading the judge, the case might have had a different outcome.

When Your Point Is Made, Stop Talking

Avoid weakening your strong point by making a weak point. This can happen even when you make a relatively minor point. If your listener disagrees with the point, she may begin to doubt everything you say, including what she was previously inclined to accept. Professional negotiators use a technique in which, after opponents have made a strong point, they simply ask if that is the opponent's only point. If the opponent responds by making a second weaker point, the negotiator aggressively attacks the weaker point, putting the opponent on the defensive. Experienced negotiators block this technique by suggesting that there is no need to consider additional points because the first point is compelling. If your first point has found the jugular and your adversary's case is critically wounded, do not revive it by giving your opponent another opportunity to attack your case.

Know When You Have Made Your Point

While some lawyers play to the gallery, others enjoy hearing themselves talk. Sometimes they continue to talk, to make yet another supposedly telling point even after the judge has acknowledged agreement with their position. By doing so, they can jeopardize their cases. These advocates would do well to remember the old adage "When you strike oil, stop boring." Many an advocate, lulled by the sound of his own voice, has snatched defeat from the jaws of victory.

Avoid Quarreling

Staying focused on your goal will help you avoid the kind of arguments that become emotionally charged battles. Some lawyers resemble George and Martha in *Who's Afraid of Virginia Woolf*, carping at one another. These verbal jousts are intended less to persuade than to wound the adversary. Usually, a self-inflicted wound results. In the early 1980s, an Indiana defense lawyer used his final argument to vent weeks of pent-up frustration in a hotly contested product liability trial. He ripped opposing counsel up one side and down the other for a series of perceived abuses and transgressions. In the process, he did little to advance his client's cause on the merits and much to alienate the jurors. They vented in return by rendering a verdict of $6 million against him. When your argument starts to sound like a quarrel, you have lost your focus on the goal and are likely to lose your argument.

Keep Your Eye on the Goal

Whatever goal you identify, never lose sight of it during your argument, regardless of temptations or distractions that may come your way. To execute tennis strokes effectively, you must always keep your eye on the ball. To make a successful argument, you must keep your eye on the goal of your argument. In a hard-fought trial, this is not always easy. To help, you might want to take a tip from a prominent Irish barrister named Daniel O'Connell. At trial, he kept a piece of paper in view at counsel's table on which he had written these words: "A good speech is a good thing, but never forget that the verdict is the thing."[3]

NOTES

1. James Russell Lowell, *Democracy and Other Addresses* (1887) (1999, Reprint Services Corporation).

2. *See* Stephen E. Toulmin, *The Uses of Argument* (1983, Cambridge University Press).

3. Richard Du Cann, *The Art of the Advocate* p. 150 (1965, MacGibbon and Kee).

Secret 2 Tailor Your Argument to the Decision-Maker

An argument is a communication. Like any communication, it includes four basic components:

1. A sender who encodes a message (a speaker)
2. The message itself
3. The medium by which the message is conveyed (oral speech, writing, television, etc.)
4. The audience that receives, decodes, and provides feedback on the message.

When you make an argument, those who receive your message are decision-makers—judges, jurors, arbitrators. They will determine the winner and the loser. In thinking about your argument, remember that of all the components of the communication process, the receiver is the most important because the receiver makes the decision.

What is persuasive to one decision-maker will often not be persuasive to another. When representing a client, you will argue at various times to a judge (on a motion), to a jury (at trial), or to the opposing party (in negotiating a settlement). In each of these arguments, your ultimate goal is the same—to get the best result possible for your client. However, even when the issue and the ultimate goal are the same, your argument in each setting will need to change because of differences among these decision-makers. What will persuade a particular judge will often be different from what will persuade a jury, and what will persuade the opposing party can be an entirely different argument altogether.

Understand Your Audience

In England during the nineteenth century, James Scarlett was a great figure at the bar. It was said that the secret of his success was that he blended his mind with the minds of the jurors. Their thoughts were his thoughts. As one juror remarked of him, "He is a lucky one, because he is always on the right side."[1] He scored victories because there were "twelve Scarletts in the jury box." Across the Atlantic in the United States during the same time period, the luminary at the American bar was Daniel Webster. The secret of his success was that ". . . by addressing the understanding of common men . . . I must use language perfectly intelligible to them. You will, therefore, find in my speeches to juries no hard words, no Latin phrases, no *fieri facias*, and that is the secret of my style."[2]

Tailor your argument. Both of these lawyers achieved greatness at least in part because they understood their audiences. More than that, they understood that their success as lawyers depended on how well they tailored their arguments to the particular audience they sought to persuade. Both Scarlett and Webster possessed an uncommon ability to make arguments that would have maximum appeal to their listeners. Whenever you argue, you should strive to do likewise.

A story is told that some years ago, an Irish barrister was arguing before the high court of Great Britain. During the argument, a member of the court commented, "I'm sure your client is familiar with the doctrine of *res ipsa loquitur*." The lawyer responded, "Yes my Lord, in Killarney where my client tends his flock of sheep, they speak of little else." Clearly, the judge in this anecdote misunderstood the litigant. You should never make the same mistake in assessing your listeners, the decision-makers.

Adopt a Receiver-Centered Approach

Consider how audiences process information. It is a mistake to think of your audience as a passive receptacle for your argument. The audience is, in fact, an active participant in the communication process.[3] When you choose words to communicate an idea, you are engaging in a process of encoding. Your listener, in turn, must decode what you have said.[4] In performing this decoding function, your audience is as much involved in creating the meaning of the communication as you are. When you speak the word "home," you may in your own mind be conjuring the idea of a quiet cottage with a green lawn and a white picket fence. To your listener, though, the same word might induce thoughts of a cramped apartment in an urban high rise.

When you argue, it is your task to induce in your listener's mind a mental picture that corresponds as closely as possible to the idea in your own mind. Never assume that your audience will understand words or concepts exactly as you do. Even with a common language, some meaning is lost in the translation from what you encode as a speaker to what your audience decodes. As an advocate, your concern must always be with the thought that will be in your listeners' minds after decoding your words.

Consider how audiences differ. Aristotle believed that the "whole affair of rhetoric is the impression to be made upon an audience."[5] Modern communications scholars make the same point when they speak of adopting a "receiver-centered" approach to persuasion.[6] They instruct speakers to focus on their audiences and to recognize that audiences differ: what works in persuading an accountant may not work in persuading a poet.

Consider human nature. The success of an argument depends on the receiver's response. To influence that response, an arguer must understand the nature of the people he wishes to persuade. The speaker "must know human nature, with its ways of reasoning, its habits, desires, and emotions, and must know the kind of argument that will persuade each kind of men, as also the emotional appeal that will gain their assent; every detail, the choice of the individual words and phrases, the arrangement of larger and smaller parts, each single item in the speech is to be determined by its effect upon the soul."[7]

Consider All Factors That Influence the Receiver's Decision

Consider preexisting factors. There are many factors that may influence the souls of the audience who will decide the fate of your client. To frame the best argument, each of these factors should be clearly understood. Subsequent chapters of this book address in depth several of the most significant factors that influence decisions, including cognitive reasons for making a particular decision (Secret 4, Base Your Argument on Reasons), the role emotions play (Secret 6, Appeal to Emotion), and the way an argument is structured or framed (Secret 8, Strategically Arrange Your Arguments). In a very real sense, everything that is discussed in this book concerns factors that influence decisions. This section addresses factors in preexisting circumstances that are not directly part of the substantive argument but that nonetheless play influential roles in decision-making. If you present your argument without understanding these factors, you are like a traveler walking in unknown territory without a map.

Consider the receiver's attitudes. Attitudes are predispositions to think or behave in a particular way. They are generally based on prior experiences. A person who has suffered from police brutality may dislike police officers and be predisposed to reject an argument that relies on police testimony. Attitudes can be analyzed in the following three dimensions: (1) direction—favorable, unfavorable, or neutral; (2) intensity—strength of the attitude (the more intense the attitude, the harder it will be to change); and (3) salience—perceived importance of the attitude to the person (the lower the salience, the less it affects behavior).

If you wanted to convince a decision-maker that O. J. Simpson committed murder, your task would be harder if the decision-maker's attitude about police officers was unfavorable (direction), strongly held (intensity), and significant to her (salience). If your listener's attitude were the opposite in any of the dimensions, your task would be easier. In fact, the difference in jurors' attitudes about police is believed to be one of the most important reasons why O. J. Simpson was acquitted of murder in his criminal trial but found responsible in the civil case.

Consider the receiver's beliefs. Belief is the degree of truth a person assigns to something. What an audience believes will often determine its decision about an issue. Like attitude, a belief possesses the dimensions of direction (ranging from complete belief to complete disbelief), intensity (the certainty with which the belief is held, from very certain to very uncertain), and salience. The salience of a belief usually depends on the circumstances. Belief in heaven may be moderately salient to a person in normal times and become highly salient when the person faces imminent death.

You may sometimes imagine that jurors start with a blank slate and are influenced only by what is presented to them at trial. In fact, all jurors and other decision-makers bring to an argument a set of beliefs acquired during a lifetime. Sometime, these beliefs will disqualify a person from serving as a decision-maker, such as when a prospective juror in a capital punishment case acknowledges not believing in the death penalty. Even when not amounting to reasons for disqualification, the wide range of preexisting beliefs that influence a decision must be taken into account in crafting your argument.

Use Care in Expressing Divergent Attitudes and Beliefs

The favorable attitudes and beliefs of an audience are like a bank account on which you as an advocate can draw. The favorable attitudes and beliefs can be cashed in to help influence belief on matters to which the audience may be initially adverse or neutral. As with a bank account, you should make deposits and avoid excessive withdrawals. You make deposits by building upon favorable attitudes and beliefs. When you express views that are extremely divergent from those of your audience, the account may become overdrawn, causing a boomerang effect—the audience not only fails to be persuaded but also strengthens its preexisting attitudes and beliefs.

One tactic for reducing this risk might be to shift responsibility for the divergent view by explaining that the adverse facts supporting that view come not from you or your client, but from independent witnesses and the written record. In this way, you direct hostile reactions away from you and your position. These considerations hold true in a mediation setting as well. If you present your strongest argument at the outset of a mediation session, it may diverge sharply from the view of the opposing party. The effect may be to harden his opposition. Similarly, if there is significant evidence calling into question the credibility or integrity of the opposing party, consider holding back this ammunition. Instead of risking a hostile reaction by the opposing party at the very outset of the mediation, advise the mediator about the evidence in a private session and let the mediator choose the time and best way of addressing the issue.

Consider the receiver's values. Values are core beliefs that are deeply felt as important to life. Belief in the values of truth, justice, fairness, family, and the like provide a foundation upon which many decisions are based. These core values represent highly salient beliefs that will often be critical to the reception of the arguments you make as a lawyer. Some of the best themes of arguments are founded on such values. For example, in *Pennzoil v. Texaco*, plaintiff's counsel relied on the theme "your word is your bond" to win a judgment of $10 billion.

Understand how the receiver's mind strives for consistency. The human mind tends to pay closer attention to, and have better recall of, messages consistent with preexisting attitudes and beliefs. As a result of this subconscious process, preexisting values tend to be reinforced and harder to change. Nevertheless, change can occur when inconsistencies arise in a person's beliefs and attitudes. The mind strives to return to a state of consistency called homeostasis and adjusts accordingly. For example, an audience may initially have a favorable attitude toward you as a speaker but an unfavorable attitude toward a position you are arguing. Over time, the audience will move to a more favorable attitude toward your position but a less favorable attitude toward you. Inconsistent attitudes tend to move toward each other.

Consider filtering effects. The human mind often acts subconsciously like a filter, easily allowing in those ideas that are consistent with preexisting attitudes and beliefs but filtering out those that are divergent. For example, in defending a product liability claim, you might consider emphasizing the fact that the product was made by

Consider Personality and Psychological Differences

One of the key factors affecting the outcome of a trial will be the personality of the decision-maker. Some people make decisions based more on how they feel than on what they think. Such people are called "left-brain" or "affective" thinkers; they tend to be creative and include the poets and artists of the world. Other personality types focus more on facts and their logical implications. These people are "right-brain" or "cognitive" thinkers and include most accountants, engineers, and lawyers. Some lawyers make the mistake of assuming that all jurors will be cognitive thinkers, especially if they themselves are. When they lose, these lawyers often criticize the jury as stupid or inept. Instead, the problem may reside with the lawyers for failing to understand the personalities of the decision-makers and adjust their arguments accordingly.

Just as one argument may persuade an artist but not an engineer, another may appeal more to judges than to juries. For example, you make an argument that your client should be acquitted of violating the water pollution statute because the pollutant, though dangerous, is technically not defined within the statute. This kind of argument may well be more persuasive to a judge than to a lay jury because, as a group, judges are more inclined to be logical thinkers. No doubt, this natural inclination is reinforced during law school, when impressionable young minds are taught to "think like lawyers."

skilled German craftsmen. If your listener is Jewish, however, with relatives who were victims of the Holocaust, the point may meet with subconscious resistance, and, in effect, be filtered out of positive consideration. On the other hand, if the judge owns a Mercedes and thinks that it is the best car ever made, she might readily accept the point.

Consider organizational interests and procedures. Decision-makers are sometimes part of an organization whose interests have the potential to influence the outcome of disputes. In *The Essence of Decision*, Graham Allison analyzed the factors that influenced President John F. Kennedy's decision to respond to the introduction of offensive nuclear missiles into Cuba in 1962. Allison found that this critical decision was influenced not only by consideration of the risks and benefits of the various policy options, but also by standard operating procedures of the Defense Department and by organizational interests of the Central Intelligence Agency.[8] Similarly, when you seek to persuade a corporation, government agency, or even the head of a family, there may be organizational interests that you should consider.

For example, in making a decision about a settlement proposal, a corporation may be influenced by both an objective calculation of settlement value and other corporate interests. These may include keeping key personnel focused on corporate priorities rather than being entangled in discovery or avoiding the establishment of an adverse legal precedent that could affect future business disputes. Mentioning these factors in a negotiation could be as persuasive as anything you might say on the merits of your claim. Corporate decisions may also be affected by internal procedures for decision-making, for example, requirements that a special committee with representatives from legal, claims, and operations decide all matters involving more than a certain monetary amount. In such circumstances, instead of just presenting your settlement argument orally to counsel, consider submitting a settlement brochure that can be shared with all members of the committee. In this way, you deliver your argument directly to all decision-makers without filtering or translation by opposing counsel.

Investigate the Decision-Maker

Generally, when you think about conducting investigations for purposes of your argument, your focus is on the facts and law that are directly relevant to the matter in dispute. In light of the factors discussed above, it should now be abundantly clear that your pre-argument investigation must extend beyond the substance of the dispute and include investigating the decision-maker. The more you know about the decision-maker's attitudes, beliefs, values, organization, personality, and background, the more effective an argument you can fashion.

INVESTIGATE JUDGES

If you are preparing to argue a case before the court, there are a variety of ways to learn specific information about who will decide your case.

Read prior opinions and writings. By reading relevant opinions or other writings, you can gain an appreciation of the judge's views. If those views differ from your position, you need to know that before presenting your argument so that you can work with or around the judge's views. You might confront the issue by stating to the judge, "I realize, Your Honor, that in the *Jackson Savings and Loan* case you opined that a breach of a fiduciary obligation is not an independent cause of action. Nevertheless, there are compelling reasons why you should consider modifying your view in this particular case. . . ." This way, you signal to the judge that you know and respect her view but that you want her to listen to your presentation with a mindset hospitable toward modification. Think of the potential embarrassment if you simply started arguing your point without acknowledging your awareness of the court's standing on a particular point.

Your ethos may be called into serious question unless the court believes you are knowledgeable, especially about the judge's perspective on the particular issue at hand. [*See* Secret 3, Cultivate Ethos.] Moreover, by acknowledging that you are aware of the court's prior ruling and by showing respect for that ruling, you establish a common point for launching your argument. Keep in mind that you sometimes may not want to attempt to persuade a judge to change a viewpoint because you believe the task is hopeless. In that event, you should focus on establishing the proper record for appellate review.

Contact people familiar with the judge. Reading prior opinions of the court does not provide insight into the mannerisms, style, and idiosyncrasies you will encounter in the judge presiding over your case. For example, will the judge be receptive to your moving away from the lectern? Will she have read your brief before oral argument? How much time should you devote to the facts or to the questions presented? Does the judge have a long or short attention span? Does he pepper counsel with many questions? In criminal cases, does the judge appear to favor the government or the defense? In civil cases, does she appear to favor the plaintiff or the defendant? You will want to know the answers to these types of questions before you present—and indeed before you plan—your argument. One effective way to get this type of information is to talk to the judge's law clerks, if the judge has no objections; to other courthouse personnel; or to lawyers who have argued before the judge.

By educating yourself about the judge's particular approach to the arguments presented by others, you gain valuable information to help you tailor your argument. For example, suppose you learn from a previous law clerk that the judge disdains lengthy pleadings. Unfortunately, your complaint is very lengthy. You might solve the dilemma in the following manner: When court convenes and the judge asks, "Is there any business to discuss before we proceed?", answer, "No, your Honor, except that I want to apologize to the court for the length of the complaint. Because this case is the subject of parallel proceedings in two other jurisdictions, we were compelled to present many facts that ordinarily would have been omitted." The effect of counsel's comment is to confront the court's concern in a pleasant manner before the judge ever addresses the issue. The result has several benefits: counsel's ethos is enhanced, and common ground with the judge is established. [*See* Secret 3, Cultivate Ethos.]

In any event, when discussing a judge with others, always take care to avoid criticism of the judge. In a recent case involving complex issues of family law, two lawyers were in the courtroom before the judge entered, and one asked the other his opinion of the judge in domestic cases. The lawyer responded that the judge was in "over his head in this case" and that counsel would have to "spoon-feed the judge" and then hold his breath. The judge overheard the comments because the internal video and audio systems were in operation at the time. The judge soundly rebuked the lawyer, and relations between them suffered considerably.

Observe the judge in other proceedings. There is no substitute for firsthand knowledge. Therefore, if you are presenting a case before a judge for the first time, make every effort to observe the judge in action in several cases. Note the judge's style, what he seems to like and dislike, how he relies on other cases. Then, tailor your presentation to the judge's preferences.

Honor Your Judge's Preferences

Bear in mind that when you talk to clerks and others about a judge, the matter can be delicate. You may not want to call current clerks of a presiding judge ex parte or ask questions that might give the impression that you are being disrespectful or bothersome, or trying to curry favor. On the other hand, some judges encourage such calls to members of their staffs. For example, a trial judge in Maryland did not approve of counsel standing when the jury entered or exited. The judge made clear that calls to his chambers regarding his preferences were most welcome and could help avoid the embarrassment of being scolded in front of the jury for breaches of preferred courtroom conduct. Other judges resent calls to chambers by counsel to inquire about their preferences.

Consider the example of a young trial lawyer defending a criminal assault case. The complaining witness had also filed a civil suit against the defendant, and defense counsel had learned that if the civil case settled, the complaining witness would not proceed with the criminal case. The defendant was adamant that he was not guilty and refused to pay the complaining witness "one red cent." The case was a close one and could have gone either way. In the particular jurisdiction, cases of this nature are often resolved by the judge, who can find the defendant guilty and impose "probation before judgment," which means placing the defendant on probation for a limited period of time. When the probationary period expires, the conviction record is erased, and no permanent criminal record is established.

The problem for the young lawyer was that, notwithstanding the "probation before judgment" option, a finding of guilty would result in considerable adverse publicity for his client. The lawyer spent two afternoons in court observing the judge and learned the judge was impatient with opening statements but was very attentive during closing arguments. He also learned that the judge rarely ruled in favor of the defendant and that, in four assault cases in which the issue of guilt was questionable, the judge found each of the defendants guilty but granted probation before judgment. After these observations, the lawyer was understandably pessimistic about the likelihood of a not-guilty finding. Based on his advice, the client agreed to settle the civil case and, with the complaining witness's consent, the criminal case was dismissed. Had this young lawyer not observed the judge in action, he probably would have tried the criminal case and had a much less desirable outcome for his client.

INVESTIGATE JURORS

There are a number of ways you can develop knowledge about jurors.

Obtain a jury list. Whenever possible, obtain the jury list in advance of trial. If a current list is not available, consider reviewing the latest list used. By reviewing the list, you can learn about the types of people you might find on your jury. For example, you may observe that many of those on the list are retired farmers, or nurses, or teachers, as opposed to business people. This knowledge will help you tailor your argument to your listener.

Use standard jury questionnaires. In many jurisdictions, in addition to the limited information available from a jury list, each prospective juror completes standard questionnaires that will provide more details about the person's background. These questionnaires should be studied carefully, not only to determine whom to select for the jury but also to help guide the presentation of your case.

Never underestimate the value of voir dire. Voir dire is the traditional way to learn about prospective jurors. Nevertheless, in many jurisdictions today, courts do not permit lawyers to conduct individual voir dire. Where individual voir dire is permitted, you should take extensive time to evaluate your case and to determine the types of people you think would be not only best suited for the case but also most harmful. In many instances you may find yourself in the position of "unpicking the jury" (i.e., identifying the two or three worst jurors and seeking to remove them).

Develop a Case-Specific Jury Questionnaire

In significant cases, give serious consideration to developing a case-specific questionnaire directed to juror attitudes, beliefs, values, and experiences relevant to the issues in the case. In most jurisdictions, the attorneys for either party can request such questionnaires, they can be prepared by one party or jointly by all parties, and they can be done with or without the assistance of jury consultants. As long as the questions are not slanted and inquire only about appropriate matters, many judges will allow them. They see the questionnaire as a way to reduce the court time required for voir dire.

Regardless of whether you participate in individual voir dire or the judge asks the questions based on counsels' written suggestions, consider asking or proposing questions that are indirect and that camouflage your real goal. Asking, "Is any member of the jury panel biased against the police?" may not elicit the same information as asking "Have you or has anyone close to you ever been arrested or charged with a crime?" In light of preceding suggestions that your arguments should be tailored to the decision-maker, never take voir dire for granted. From voir dire, you gain information to help you select a jury and to shape your argument.

Conducting skillful voir dire is an art. You must study the subject, practice developing your skill, and never undertake it without careful planning. Unfortunately, many arguments are lost because the wrong juror was selected. You should try to prevent this from occurring by asking the proper voir dire questions to expose and eliminate those with a bias that even the best argument will not be able to overcome.

Conduct jury research. The business world has long recognized the value of market research. Before deciding to air a new commercial or to launch a new product on which millions of dollars may ride, marketing professionals make a concerted effort to find out how the prospective audience is likely to respond. These professionals do not rely, as many lawyers do, on gut instinct, prior experience, or the advice of a colleague or friend. Instead, they exploit tools of the behavioral sciences, including survey research, focus groups, and experimental testing. They make decisions based on collected data that has been scientifically analyzed. These same tools are available to you and, in an appropriate case, can produce significant information that could influence the outcome of your case.

Submit Jury Questions

If the judge in your case does not permit individual voir dire, do not offer a few last-minute questions. Prepare your questions in advance. When the judge announces at the outset that she expects to have the jury seated in five minutes, submit your proposed questions and, if the judge does not ask them, remember to make your proffer to preserve the record.

Use jury consultants. To conduct effective jury research, you will often need the assistance of a professional jury consultant who is trained to conduct and analyze behavioral research. The cases most appropriate for such research are those involving unusual complexity or high stakes, such as a multiple death case arising from a plane crash in which the defendant manufacturer is alleged to have designed and built a defective light aircraft.

In just such a case, the defense relied on a jury consultant to provide guidance on how best to demonstrate to the jury that the aircraft was airworthy. Three alternatives were evaluated: a film showing the aircraft; jury inspection of the aircraft at a local airport hangar; and a model of the aircraft. A study performed with three matched groups of mock jurors who were respectively shown the film, the actual plane, or the model indicated, surprisingly, that the model plane was the most helpful of the alternatives. The actual plane produced a negative response because the jurors regarded it as frighteningly insubstantial, and the presence of oil and grease stains on the tarmac heightened their fears. Based on this study, the model was selected for use in court and contributed to a verdict for the defense.

Develop jury profiles. Another effective use of a jury consultant is to help select or strike prospective jurors. A consultant, relying on data developed by surveys, interviews, and focus groups, can profile the types of jurors who are likely to be receptive to your argument. The consultant can then assist you at trial in recognizing which prospective jurors best fit the profile.

Use a "shadow" jury. In some cases, a consultant may recruit a "shadow jury" to watch the actual proceedings as if they were the jury. The consultant can get daily feedback from the shadow jury on issues such as what seemed confusing, what worked well, and what did not. One of the unique benefits of this process is that the shadow jury can indicate what they would like to know about the case when you still have an opportunity to make changes in your presentation.

Conduct a mock trial. Another helpful tool to learn how jurors may react to your argument is a mock trial. Here, you present your case before a consultant and a group of private citizens recruited to hear the case, render a verdict, and participate with you and the consultant in a discussion about the case. Recruits are selected from the community who are likely to match the types of people who will be on the actual jury. When you present the case, colleagues in your office can play opposing counsel, and actors or staff members can be witnesses. If you have the facilities, it is very informative to watch the deliberations through a one-way mirror. If there is no one-way mirror available, put a camera in a corner of the room and videotape the deliberation for later review.

Conduct mock trial post-verdict interviews. After the verdict, meet with the jurors and seek constructive criticism. The consultant can ask questions of the group to help you understand how the jurors reacted and what additional information they might have wanted. You can then reshape your argument for presentation to the actual jury. In one such exercise the mock jurors complained that they would have liked photographs of several of the buildings involved in the dispute and wanted to hear from a witness counsel had chosen not to call. In the actual trial, counsel followed the wishes of the mock jurors and ultimately prevailed in the case.

Understand the limits of jury research. Of course, hiring a jury consultant does not guarantee a successful result. There are, in fact, some self-styled jury consultants whose work is not scientific and whose guidance is, in reality, no better than what you might receive from a stranger selected at random. Sometimes, even well-conducted jury research will prove to be of minimal value, such as when the jury that is seated through no fault of the consultant bears little resemblance to the group that was surveyed. Nevertheless, properly conducted, jury research can often provide enlightening information about your audience that will enable you to develop and deliver a more effective presentation.

Check out the internet. The internet is a font of information about virtually everything, including information about judges and jurors. Typically, a search on the web about any person begins with a search engine such as google.com, yahoo.com, dogpile .com, or ask.com. The difficult part of using these search engines is that they often yield too many results. The key to successfully searching the web is to use techniques to narrow your search results. You can do this in a variety of ways, depending on what, precisely, you need.

A good technique is to use synonyms, or Boolean logic. For example, if you are looking for information regarding Judge John Q. Justice, and you type *"John Q. Justice" AND Judge* into the search box, the results would be much narrower than if you had simply typed *John Q. Justice*. Searching within parentheses will provide results that contain the exact phrase. By capitalizing *AND*, your results will consist of information pertaining to both terms, "*John Q. Justice*" AND *Judge*.

Some websites charge a fee to access their information. Search engines cannot search websites that require passwords and/or subscriptions, such as databases like westlaw.com and accruint .com. Most such databases require subscriptions, and they can cost a considerable amount of money. However, these databases provide a vast amount of information. In Westlaw or Lexis, for example, you can quickly access every published opinion authored by your judge.

It is often useful to check out the website for your particular court. Such websites may contain biographical information about your judge as well as other background information about the court that may be instructive. You can also search the website of the newspaper that covers the court for news articles pertaining to the judge or potential jurors. In many areas, there are blogs that focus on a particular courthouse or jurisdiction that can be enlightening. Another way of finding information on a specific person is to browse social networking groups like LinkedIn, MySpace, or Facebook.

Sometimes an internet search will provide no useful information, and other times you may find a treasure trove, like a lengthy in-depth interview with your judge or a website created by a juror describing her interests. Before you place too much stock on any information found on the web, make sure that the source is reliable. The vast content of cyberspace is unregulated and there is much that is not true.

Focus on the Most Persuadable Decision-Makers

Where your investigation reveals that your case has no chance of success with some of the decision-makers, consider pitching your case to those who may be more amenable to your points. This technique should be used only in those rare circumstances when you are sure that the cause is hopeless with those you are (politely) ignoring. The great English barrister Edward Carson once found himself in this position. In the midst of argument to an appellate court, Judge Lawson blurted out roughly, "Mr. Carson, you've got no case." Carson, unperturbed, continued for another twenty minutes, only to be interrupted again by Lawson, who said, "Mr. Carson, I say you've got no case." Carson then turned politely to Lawson and responded, "My Lord, I heard you say that twenty minutes ago and knew it would be useless to argue the merits of my case with your Lordship. Since then I have not addressed one word to your Lordship; I've been addressing the other judges, and may I be allowed to go on without your Lordship's interruption."[9] While you would rarely, if ever, address the court as Carson did, you may want to adopt his strategy by directing your argument to those most likely to accept it.

Adjust Your Presentation to Audience Feedback

Be alert for clues. During arguments, judges, jurors, and other decision-makers often provide feedback about the matters being addressed. This feedback may be verbal, such as when a judge poses a question. More often, the feedback is nonverbal, in the form of a quizzical facial expression, a nod, a scowl, a yawn, arms folded across the chest, a smile, or any number of cues. Although providing valuable information, this feedback is frequently missed by lawyers who focus solely on their prepared arguments as if they were wearing blinders.

Watch the case. In his classic work on cross-examination, Francis Wellman tells a story about Sir Charles Russell of Killowen, who "was altogether the most successful cross-examiner of modern times."

Respond to Your Listener's Cues

When your listener indicates by a facial expression that she is confused on a point, instead of continuing on to the next point as planned, take more time to flesh out the point more fully. When your listener yawns, try to increase interest by changing your pace, moving away from the lectern, or addressing a more compelling point. When your listener shakes her head or frowns in response to a point, try a different tack, perhaps drawing on an anecdote or affirming your listener's response. For example, you might say: "I can certainly understand why a person might be skeptical when hearing a claim like this. On first impression, it does seem a little far-fetched. But when you take a closer look, you'll find it makes sense. Allow me to explain . . ." Whatever nonverbal cues you receive from your audience, take them into account as you proceed with your argument. In a conversation with someone, you would routinely respond to verbal feedback. Similarly, in argument you should respond to nonverbal feedback by adjusting your argument.

Russell was in a trial with a junior lawyer who was taking notes in the orthodox fashion. Russell was taking no notes and instead was thoroughly on the alert, glancing about the court at the judge, the jury, the witness, or counsel on the other side. Suddenly, he turned to the junior and asked "What are you doing?" "Taking a note," was the response. Russell burst out, "What the devil do you mean by saying you are taking a note? Why don't you watch the case?" Russell had been "watching" the case. When something happened to make a change of attack necessary, "he wheeled his colleagues around almost before they had time to grasp the new situation."[10] By watching and listening to your listener, you can often obtain valuable clues as to what your listener is thinking. These clues can then be used to adjust your argument to give it maximum appeal.

Avoid overinterpreting. Your listener's nonverbal behavior will not always indicate what he is thinking. Not every wink or nod is a message. When a juror crosses his arms, he may be signaling that he does not like what you said, or it may be merely that he is cold. When a judge leans back and away from you, she may be rejecting your point, or it could be that she is just tired of leaning forward. A frown could indicate displeasure with your argument, or it might reflect a sore back. There is no dictionary for nonverbal communication because there is no universal meaning for specific behaviors. Beware of charlatans who claim otherwise. Even when the meaning seems clear, you could be wrong. Consider, for example, the juror who repeatedly smiled at defense counsel during a trial and nodded affirmatively when counsel was making crucial points. After a favorable verdict, counsel sought this juror out to thank her, only to learn that she had strongly opposed the defense position and had acquiesced in the verdict reluctantly after a long and arduous deliberation. Asked to explain why she had been smiling and nodding, she responded that she was just being polite. The lesson is this: do not ignore nonverbal feedback, but be cautious in interpreting its meaning. [For further analysis of nonverbal communication, *see* Secret 10, Use Delivery to Enhance Communication.]

Seek to have your listener identify with you. Research has confirmed that listeners are more easily persuaded by speakers whom they perceive to be similar to themselves. Kenneth Burke is regarded by many as the preeminent writer on rhetoric in the twentieth century, in part because of his recognition of the powerful role that the concept of identification plays in persuasion. Burke observed, "You persuade a man only insofar as you can talk his language by speech, gesture, tonality, order, image, attitude, idea, identifying your ways with his." You persuade more effectively when you show yourself to be a fellow member of your listener's tribe.[11]

Establish common ground. Psychologists have found that we trust and like people who are like us. That is why, when they go to Iowa, politicians talk about their connections to farming. Similarly, in the Oklahoma City bombing trial of Terry Nichols, defense counsel Michael Tigar commiserated with one prospective juror about their common ordeal of raising teenagers. With a former French exchange student, he talked about France, and with a poet he talked about poetry. By doing so, he made connections with these jurors that lasted throughout the trial—connections that undoubtedly contributed to the jury foreperson's opinion that "Michael Tigar is one heck of an attorney." Not coincidentally, Tigar avoided the death penalty for his client. Though logically irrelevant to the issues to be tried, discussing matters of common experience can help your listener to identify with you and to become more receptive to your arguments.

Find a Higher Level Issue That Appeals to Your Listener

Establish the importance of the decision to be made. When you tell a friend that you have a serious matter to discuss that affects many people beyond just the two of you, the attention level of your friend immediately rises. When you gain this type of attention, you enhance your opportunity to communicate. Similarly, when you elevate the importance of the issues in your case, you increase your persuasive opportunities. You engage your listener and give your listener a feeling of importance because you are presenting your case as a significant one that affects the community beyond the courtroom. People enjoy doing meaningful work. Creating an important issue for your listener to decide helps you to establish rapport and get your listener's attention.

Identify a universal theme. You can be particularly effective if you can elevate the theme of your case to a universal theme that is consistent with the attitudes and beliefs of your listeners. You can create the atmosphere of an important case and, at the same time, indicate that your view of the best resolution of the case is just like your listeners'. The goal is to have your listeners identify with you and look to you as their leader. You create a bond with your listeners and prime them to help you. For example, if a jury is composed mostly of factory workers, a case involving an escalator accident can be premised on a theme that affects them all.

In such circumstances, counsel would go beyond the narrow facts of the case. Counsel's opening statement might begin like this: "Ladies and Gentlemen, this case is not only about Johnny Roger's broken leg caused by the failure of the escalator, it is also about the need for American manufacturers to make products that are safe for public use. Safety in industry is a big problem in America today. If the GPA Company had not abandoned standards of safety, this tragedy would not have occurred. . . ." Counsel in this example knew that the jurors would be very safety conscious. Elevating the issue to a universal theme consistent with your listeners' views creates a positive relationship between you and them.

Frame issues in emotionally compelling terms. In the 1970 trial of the Chicago Seven,[12] William Kuntsler represented clients who had deliberately offended the judge and jury in almost every conceivable way. In closing argument, Kuntsler did not limit himself to arguing whether the evidence proved his clients guilty of the charged offenses of conspiracy to cross state lines to incite a riot. Instead, he framed the issue in terms of "the right of men to think, the right of men to speak boldly and unafraid, the right to be masters of their souls, and the right to live free and die free." He called the courtroom a "proving ground of whether we do live free and we do die free." In this way, he associated his otherwise unappealing clients with values that the jury would find emotionally compelling.[13]

Associate your case with your listener's values. Whenever you argue, search for a way to connect your client's specific situation with the fundamental values of your listener. If you can find such a connection, you will be well on your way to achieving the same kind of mutuality with your listeners as did James Scarlett who, as noted at the beginning of this chapter, blended his own mind with those of his listeners.

NOTES

1. *See* Lloyd Paul Stryker, *The Art of Advocacy* p. 56 (1956, Corner Stone Library).

2. Robert Remini, *Daniel Webster, the Man and His Time* p. 80 (1997, W. W. Norton).

3. Thomas Murphy, "Maintaining Effective Juror Communication," *For the Defense* p. 25 (January 1999).

4. Donald E. Vinson and David S. Davis, *Jury Persuasion: Psychological Strategies and Trial Techniques* (1996, Glasser LegalWorks).

5. Lane Cooper, translator, *The Rhetoric of Aristotle* (1934, Prentice-Hall).

6. *See e.g.*, James C. McCroskey, *An Introduction to Rhetorical Communication* (7th ed.) pp. 25, 155 (1996, Allyn and Bacon).

7. Lane Cooper, translator, *The Rhetoric of Aristotle* (1934, Prentice-Hall).

8. Graham T. Allison, *The Essence of Decision: Explaining the Cuban Missile Crisis* pp. 125, 190 (1971, Little, Brown and Company).

9. Edward Marjoribanks, *The Life of Lord Carson* p. 29 (1932, McMillan Company).

10. Francis L. Wellman, *The Art of Cross-Examination* pp. 183–184 (1903) (Reprint 1998, MacMillan Publishing Company).

11. Kenneth Burke, *A Rhetoric of Motives* p. 55 (1969, University of California Press).

12. *State of Illinois v. Abbie Hoffman, et al.*, Chicago, Illinois, February 1970.

13. The full argument is reported in Michael S. Lief, H. Mitchell Caldwell, and Benjamin Bycel, *Ladies and Gentlemen of the Jury: Greatest Closing Arguments in Modern Law* pp. 103–118 (1998, Scribner).

Secret 3 Cultivate Ethos

The perceived character of the advocate can have an enormous impact on the persuasive effect of an argument. Indeed, Aristotle believed that this factor, which he called "ethos," is the most potent factor in any argument. As a lawyer, you have little influence over the facts of your case or over the applicable law, but you can affect how your listener will perceive your character and thereby enhance the likelihood that your argument will succeed. To exploit this opportunity fully, it is helpful to understand the principal components of ethos and to consider the implications of these components in situations that you regularly confront. The qualities that contribute to ethos include honesty, integrity, intelligence, knowledge, goodwill, and sincerity.

Initial Ethos and Derived Ethos

At first blush, you might think that ethos would stand wholly apart from the argument, and in one sense it does—you have an "initial ethos" with your listener before the first word is uttered. This initial ethos may be based on what your listener has previously seen or heard about you, through a prior personal contact, by reputation, or by observing your appearance and conduct in court before you speak. During an argument, this initial ethos is subject to being changed by the content and presentation of your message, resulting in what has been called "derived ethos." In making decisions about what to argue and how to argue it, the advocate should be constantly alert to the potential implications to his or her ethos, taking steps to enhance that ethos whenever possible.

Create the Impression of Honesty and Integrity

Establish your trustworthiness. Aristotle identified the integrity of the speaker as a key component of ethos. His Roman successor as a teacher of rhetoric, Quintilian, was even more emphatic on the point. He stated, "An orator must above all things study morality, and must obtain a thorough knowledge of all that is just and honorable, without which no one can either be a good man or an able speaker."[1] When you create the impression that you are a person of honesty and integrity, you will have a considerable advantage over someone who is perceived otherwise. More recently, social science research has confirmed that when you are perceived as low in trustworthiness, it matters little how high your other credibility factors are. Your ability to persuade is significantly compromised.

Take into account the general public's view of lawyers. Research shows that if an audience is informed that the speaker has ulterior selfish motives, the speaker's persuasive ability is diminished because the audience doubts that the speaker can be trusted. Thus, those you seek to persuade will often view you, as a hired advocate, with suspicion. Indeed, the general public holds lawyers in low regard. For that reason alone, you are at a disadvantage in the race for perceived integrity and trustworthiness. Nevertheless, there are steps that you can take to diminish this suspicion and negative perception. Great lawyers like Abraham Lincoln and Daniel Webster achieved prominence at least in part because listeners perceived that what they said could be trusted.

Speak about truth and fairness. Demonstrate your concern with truth and fairness by speaking directly about these values. Do not assume that your listener will recognize your allegiance to such fundamental values. In fact, opinion polls suggest the opposite.

Minimize References to Your Role as a Lawyer

Instead of referring to the party you represent as "your client," use the client's name. Every time you say "client," you remind your listener of your role as your client's "hired gun." Of course, your listener will ordinarily realize that you are a lawyer, but you need not emphasize the point.

Speak expressly in terms of the truth of what happened and the fair and just resolution of the dispute. By speaking of truth and fairness as shared values, you reinforce in your listener's mind your own adherence to these values.

Be honest. For purposes of persuasion, it is the perception of integrity that matters. It is possible to create that perception without a basis in fact, but doing so is much harder and more uncertain. If you exercise license with the truth, you run the risk of betrayal by evidence to the contrary, by your own body language, and by subtle forms of impeachment by others such as a judge who may begin to view what you say with open skepticism.

Admit unfavorable facts. When you are forthcoming about problems or weaknesses in your case, you enhance your personal credibility. When you disclose bad facts up front, you not only minimize the adverse effect of the bad facts, you also make yourself appear more credible.

Demonstrate your sense of fair play. If a prospective juror has a clear bias in your favor that would subject her to a challenge for cause, openly stipulate that she may be excused. Though it may be to your disadvantage, demonstrating your fairness strengthens your ability to persuade the remaining jurors. Whenever an opportunity is presented, show your listener by your deeds that your expressed concern for fairness is genuine.

Avoid taking extreme positions. It is easy in the heat of a legal battle to argue your position in the strongest possible terms while belittling the opposing viewpoint. In the process, you can lose your credibility with the court. One federal judge has characterized such extremism in argument as a form of deceit and dishonesty that is far too prevalent. If you give the opposing position its due while arguing your own position in a moderate and reasonable light, your case is made most strongly, and you avoid damage to your own credibility.

Avoid asserting facts that your listener is unlikely to believe. If a listener thinks that you are speaking falsely about any fact, your credibility will be undermined, and your ability to persuade your listener about other facts or about the inferences to be drawn will be compromised. Even if you are convinced of its truth, a statement is better omitted if your listener is not likely to believe it.

Demonstrate Your Knowledge of the Issues

Create the perception of intelligence. A second factor in ethos is the perception that the speaker knows what he is talking about and, therefore, should be believed. This common-sense principle has been confirmed by research in a variety of contexts. For example, a message on radioactivity was found to be much more effective when the speaker was identified as a professor of nuclear research than when the speaker was identified as a student. Similarly, it has been confirmed that an article describing a cure for the common cold is more likely to be believed if the reader is informed that the article appeared in the *New England Journal of Medicine* rather than in *Life Magazine*. This research proves what Aristotle suggested more than 2,000 years ago, when he explained the importance of intelligence as an element in ethos. A speaker who is perceived as intelligent and knowledgeable will generally be more persuasive. How do you create that perception? There are several approaches.

Organize logically. How you structure your argument will affect the impression you make on your listener. If your points are made haphazardly without consideration of their order and their relationship to one another, your listener will question your understanding of the matter. Take the time to develop a coherent order so that your points are presented in a logical sequence. [*See* Secret 8, Strategically Arrange Your Arguments.] In helping your listener to understand your argument, you will also enhance your ethos.

Explain the source of your facts. When relying on facts in an argument, it is usually helpful to describe how you came to learn them. For example, you may explain that you know the witness had been drinking because during pretrial discovery, the witness admitted in a deposition that he drank a six-pack of beer shortly before the accident. By providing this kind of information, you demonstrate the basis for your knowledge of the case and thereby strengthen the perception that you know what you are talking about.

Corroborate what you say. Another way to create the perception of knowledge is to corroborate what you say whenever possible. For example, if you refer to contract language, show your listener the contract. If you speak of a bent fender, display a photograph of the fender. Let your listener see that there is a substantial basis for what you say. This will lend credibility to all of your statements, including those that are not easily corroborated.

Do not read your argument. It has become a fundamental principle of advocacy that you should never read your argument. One of the reasons for this principle is that if you read, you forfeit the opportunity to show your listener that you really know what you are talking about. Any fool can read a speech. To make your points

Prepare. Prepare. Prepare.

The most reliable way to appear knowledgeable to your listener is by being knowledgeable in fact. You acquire knowledge pertinent to your argument by thorough investigation and examination of each fact, each principle of law, each witness, and each document. This requires careful consideration of the strengths and weaknesses of your case—of how your opponent's strengths can be answered and your weaknesses overcome. Vincent Bugliosi, who successfully prosecuted Charles Manson, believes that thorough preparation means writing down the facts of the case in elaborate detail. In a complex case, this may require two or three hundred pages of notes. Bugliosi estimates that he spent about 600 hours preparing his opening statement and closing argument for the Manson trial.

Being articulate and quick on your feet can also give the impression of knowledge and intelligence, but in the end there is no substitute for preparation. As Louis Nizer put it, "All of the other qualities—improvisation, ebullience, resourceful thinking, felicity on your feet, and facility of expression—all of these are satellites, and they all revolve around the sun; and the sun is thorough preparation."[2]

extemporaneously requires knowledge. Extemporaneous speaking should never be confused with impromptu speaking. A good extemporaneous argument should be carefully prepared and delivered not as a dramatic reading or recitation of memorized lines but as part of a conversation. Note that being freed of a text also has the benefit of allowing better eye contact with your listener. Eye contact is helpful in promoting other ethos qualities like integrity and sincerity.

Engender Goodwill

Understand what makes a person "likable." Another factor in ethos is what Aristotle referred to as goodwill and some modern scholars have called "likability." If a listener feels goodwill toward you as a speaker, research confirms that listener is more likely to accept your argument. In fact, a survey of 600 jurors found that, along with skill, a lawyer's likability was the best predictor of verdicts.

How do you engender goodwill? Dale Carnegie identified six ways to make people like you. Although these ways are not transferable to every context in which you argue, they all have utility in some situations and are worth noting:[3]

1. Become genuinely interested in other people.
2. Smile.
3. Remember that a person's name is to that person the sweetest and most important sound in any language.
4. Be a good listener. Encourage others to talk about themselves.
5. Talk in terms of the other person's interests.
6. Make the other person feel important, and do it sincerely.

In recent years, some lawyers have been more adept at engendering ill will. In fact, the *New York Times* observed, "One reason companies lose lawsuits is that they are represented by obnoxious counsel."[4] To help you minimize the risk of appearing obnoxious, here are a few additional guidelines.

Be courteous and civil at all times. No matter how provocative the behavior of your opponent, you win nothing by abandoning common courtesy. In fact, any display of bad manners will inure to your detriment. For example, if your adversary makes an *ad hominem* attack on you, it is natural to want to respond angrily in kind. Do not stoop to your opponent's level, for you will surely harm your own ethos as you try to inflict reciprocal damage on your adversary. Refuse to be drawn into such exchanges. Discuss the matter, if at all, only to point out that a personal attack is usually the last refuge of an advocate when the facts and the law are against him. Make this retort briefly and without acrimony. Then, focus on the substance of your argument.

Never talk down to your audience. Some lawyers, trying to help a lay jury understand a legal complexity, talk down to them as if they were simpletons. Although it is critical that your argument be clear, you cannot allow your presentation to sound like a schoolteacher talking to third-graders. If the jurors get the impression that you do not respect their intelligence, irreparable damage will be done to your ethos.

Use voir dire to establish rapport with jurors. When you are lead trial counsel on a case outside your home territory you may have local counsel who would like to handle voir dire. Although local counsel may do a fine job in voir dire, you will have lost an important opportunity to establish your own rapport with individual jurors. In trial, the best opportunity to display your likability and to create goodwill with the jury is by conducting voir dire yourself.

Engage in friendly conversation. In a negotiation setting, it is also helpful to develop goodwill through friendly conversation. In a study of business negotiators, Neil Rackham found that the best negotiators consistently engaged in friendly small talk to establish rapport before knuckling down to negotiating.[5]

Avoid hostility toward your opponent. The next time you are in a hotly disputed case and are tempted to become hostile, consider this advice from Abraham Lincoln:[6]

> *It is an old and true maxim that "a drop of honey catches more flies than a gallon of gall." So with men, if you would win a man to your cause, first convince him that you are his sincere friend. Therein is a drop of honey that catches his heart; which, say what you will, is the great high road to his reason.*

Convey Your Conviction

Develop a theory of the case that you can believe. If you take a case to trial, you should have a theory that you can sincerely espouse.

If not, settle. [As to the development of a theory, *see* Secret 5, Build with Evidence, Law, and Policy.]

Speak like you mean it. To be credible, you must speak with sincerity and conviction. As Cicero explained, "Unless there be, beneath the surface, matter understood and felt by the speaker, oratory becomes an empty and almost puerile flow of words."[7] Great advocates have many different styles, but one constant is their ability to convey to the audience their personal belief in what they are saying. Edward Bennett Williams calls this the "affidavit quality of a lawyer." Show that you are personally convinced of the truth and correctness of your cause. Marshall Hall, a renowned English barrister, tells the story of hearing a jury speech that was "perfect in composition and logic, but it left one cold." After rendering a verdict adverse to the speaker, one of the jurors was asked how he had failed to be convinced by the speech. "Oh," said he, "the speech was right enough, but he didn't believe a word of it himself; he had his tongue in his cheek all the time."[8]

State only what you believe. The key to speaking like you mean it is to confine your argument to statements that you believe. As Ralph Waldo Emerson observed, "[T]hat which we do not believe, we cannot adequately say."[9]

Be yourself. Do not try to imitate anyone else's style. If you do, your body language will reveal you as a phony. [For further analysis of body language, *see* Secret 10, Use Delivery to Enhance Communication.]

Be Well Groomed

Whether a speaker is attractive can affect his ethos. Research suggests that as a general rule, the more attractive the speaker, the greater the ethos. This is why good-looking politicians tend to have an advantage over more homely challengers. It is possible, on the other hand, to be too beautiful or too handsome. Features befitting a fashion model can negatively affect other ethos factors such as intelligence, likability, and identification. Whether blessed with good looks or not, you should try to look your best whenever you are engaged in an argument. Your appearance will not usually be the most important factor in ethos, but it can play a role. [*See* Secret 10, Use Delivery to Enhance Communication.]

Be Dynamic

Show enthusiasm. The dynamism of a speaker can also contribute to ethos. Generally, the more energy and enthusiasm you show, the more likely you are to get a favorable response. Some advocates think that in order to appear lawyerly, arguments must be somber and dispassionate. This is one reason why lawyers are often thought of as boring and dull. It is, of course, important that you appear serious and intelligent, but these traits are not inconsistent with being dynamic and enthusiastic.

Show emotion. The key to dynamism is emotion. If you care about what you are saying, do not be afraid to show it. Speak with emphasis and conviction. By doing so, you not only hold your listener's attention, you enhance your ethos.

In Strategizing, Weigh All Factors, Including Ethos

In preparing any argument, there are always strategic and tactical decisions to make that could influence your ethos with your listener, either positively or negatively. In making these decisions, the potential effect on your ethos should be weighed along with other relevant factors. Consider, in particular, how the decision might affect your listener's perception of your integrity, your knowledge, and your sincerity. Consider also the effect on whether your listener will like you. As Aristotle observed long ago, and as contemporary research has confirmed, these considerations of ethos could make the difference between whether your argument succeeds or fails.

NOTES

1. J. S. Watson, editor, *Quintilian: Institutes of Oratory* XII, ii, p. 1 (1856).
2. Louis Nizer, *How to Prepare a Winning Case* in *The Trial Masters: A Handbook on Strategies and Tactics that Win Cases* pp. 3–4 (1984, Prentice-Hall), edited by Bertram Warshaw.
3. Dale Carnegie, *How to Win Friends and Influence People* (1936) (Reprint 1998, Pocket Books).
4. Quoted in "The Evidence Store" by David Owen, *The Atlantic Monthly* (April 1988) p. 62.
5. Neil Rackham, *The Psychology of Negotiating* (audio tape).
6. Quoted in Dale Carnegie, *How to Win Friends and Influence People* p. 128 (1936) (Reprint 1998, Pocket Books).
7. H. Rackham and E. W. Sutton, translators, *Cicero: De Oratore* I, 6 (1988, Harvard University Press).
8. Richard Du Cann, *The Art of the Advocate* p. 59 (1964, Pelican Books).
9. Ralph Waldo Emerson, *Essays: Essay on Spiritual Laws* p. 148 (1876).

Secret 4 Base Your Argument on Reasons

An argument without reasons is an empty vessel—it has no substance and no chance of winning. With strong reasons, an argument can become invincible. Reasons have two fundamental elements: data and logic. For your arguments as a lawyer, the data usually consist of facts, law, or policy considerations that provide the substantive content to support your position. These matters are addressed in a later chapter. [See Secret 5, Build with Evidence, Law and Policy.] In this chapter, our focus is on logic—the reasoning process by which data relates to a conclusion. Here we discuss several types of reasons based on their logical form and also consider a number of logical fallacies. Understanding these concepts can be helpful to your work as an advocate in several ways. It can facilitate discovery of reasons to support your argument that might not otherwise have occurred to you.

It can enhance your ability to attack opposing arguments by identifying their logical weaknesses. Moreover, by understanding clearly the logical basis of your own argument, you will be better able to explain your reasons and defend them from attack.

Distinguish between Inductive and Deductive Arguments

In deductive arguments, focus on the premises. Aristotle identified two fundamental forms of reasoning: inductive and deductive. With either form, there are premises that lead to a conclusion. If the conclusion follows necessarily from the premises and contains no new information, the reasoning is deductive. For example, start with the premise that all lawsuits for personal injury are barred unless filed within three years of the injury. If, as a second premise, it is established that John Jones's lawsuit was filed four years after his injury, it follows necessarily that John Jones's lawsuit is time barred. This argument is based on deductive reasoning. If the premises are true, the conclusion is always true. Thus, in a deductive argument the focus is always on the premises. Once the premises are established as true, the argument is won.

In inductive arguments, focus on the inference. When a conclusion relies upon an inference and contains new information not found in the premises, the reasoning is inductive. For example, if premises were established that the defendant slurred his words, stumbled as he walked, and smelled of alcohol, you might reasonably infer the conclusion that the defendant was drunk. This is inductive reasoning. In an inductive argument the conclusion is, at best, probable. The conclusion is not always true when the premises are true. The probability of the conclusion depends on the strength of the inference from the premises. Thus, when dealing with inductive reasoning, pay special attention to the inductive leap or inference by which the conclusion follows from the premises.

Reject popular misconceptions. There are several popular misconceptions about inductive and deductive reasoning. When Sherlock Holmes made his remarkable "deductions" based on observations of various facts, he was usually engaging in inductive, not deductive, reasoning. It is commonly thought that inductive arguments start with specific premises and come to a general conclusion, and that deductive arguments do the reverse. Although often the case, this sequencing is not always true and, therefore, does not accurately differentiate deductive and inductive reasoning. The best way to identify the underlying reasoning is to look for the two hallmarks of deductive reasoning: first, the conclusion follows necessarily from the premises; second, the conclusion contains no new information. If these hallmarks are present, the reasoning is deductive; if not, it is inductive.

Use Inductive Reasoning to Draw Conclusions from Particulars

Inductive reasoning is the dominant method of reasoning in the development of the common law. As Judge Benjamin Cardozo explained, "The common law does not work from pre-established truths of universal and inflexible validity to conclusions derived from them deductively. Its method is inductive, and it draws its generalizations from particulars."[1] Inductive reasoning is also an important way to argue your case from the evidence.

There are three principal types of inductive reasoning: (1) generalization; (2) analogy; and (3) causal correlation. These are discussed in the following sections.

Use Generalization to Infer a Probable Conclusion from Specific Instances

Identify specific examples. Generalization is a type of inductive reasoning that begins with consideration of specific instances and then infers a general conclusion from those instances. For example, evidence of several instances in which Ford Explorers were involved in rollover accidents might lead to the generalization that all Ford Explorers are susceptible to rollovers. Another example would be arguing the probable life expectancy of an injured plaintiff when the claimed life expectancy is based upon the life expectancy of other plaintiffs of similar age reflected in life expectancy tables. The use of statistical analysis or sampling in false claims and discrimination cases is still another example of inductive reasoning by generalization, as is an argument for lost profits based upon profits from prior years. Argument by generalization assumes that what is true of a sample from a class is also true of other members of that class. Its inverse is categorical syllogism, discussed later, a form of deductive argument that assumes that what is true of a class is also true of individual members of that class.

Use a sufficient number of examples. The strength of your argument by generalization depends on both the quantity and quality of the specific instances. It is important when you use argument by generalization that you consider enough examples to provide a solid basis for the inductive conclusion. Otherwise, opposing counsel can argue that "one swallow does not make a summer." Ordinarily, the fewer the instances, the weaker the generalization.

Use typical examples. If the instances are not qualitatively typical or representative of the whole class, the basis for generalizing will be weak. In 1936, a nationwide telephone poll of households indicated that President Roosevelt would lose his bid for reelection to the Republican candidate, Alf Landon. At the time, the people who had telephones were not representative of the electorate as a whole and, contrary to the poll's results, Roosevelt won in a landslide. That is why pollsters today randomly select samples from the entire spectrum of likely voters and take pains to avoid anything that would bias the sample.

Account for negative instances. Another fallacy that can occur when you use argument by generalization is the failure to account for negative instances. Examples that do not conform to the general pattern cannot be ignored. If the evidence reveals that many pit bulls are violent and a few are not (i.e., there are negative instances), it would be invalid to conclude that all pit bulls are violent. It would, on the other hand, be valid to generalize by adding an appropriate qualifying term such as "most"—"most pit bulls are violent." To make a valid argument, you must qualify the inductive argument to account for any negative instances.

Avoid the Fallacy of Hasty Generalization

When you make an inductive leap to a generalization without a sufficient sample of representative instances, you commit the logical fallacy known as hasty generalization. For example, your opponent might argue that her client's future lost profits are $2 million, based on profits from one prior year. But if that year's profits were unusually high, her generalization is based on data that is deficient in both quantity (only one instance) and quality (an atypical year). Your familiarity with the basic principles of logic will enable you to avoid this pitfall. You will also be able to spot this weakness in your opponent's argument and to attack it effectively.

Use Analogy When Two Instances Are Similar

Focus on only two instances. All inductive reasoning is based on observing similarity among a limited number of instances and then making inferences about additional unobserved instances. With induction by generalization, your focus is on a single characteristic that is observed among the sample instances. In the pit bull example, based on instances of violence among observed pit bulls, you infer that the same characteristic exists in unobserved pit bulls. With induction by analogy, you compare like cases, focusing on a very few specific instances, usually only two. If they are alike in several relevant characteristics, induction by analogy would suggest that they will be alike in a characteristic that is known in one instance but not in the other. You would be arguing by analogy if during mediation, you were to cite a jury verdict in a prior case that is like yours in all material respects. Because the prior case resulted in a jury verdict of $250,000, you infer that your case would have a similar result at trial and, therefore, should have a settlement value of $250,000. Another example is arguing that known roof defects in buildings number six and seven also exist in building number eight because both roofs were constructed by the same company, using the same materials and the same personnel.

Use analogical reasoning when arguing from precedent. Reasoning by analogy is frequently used in arguments of law. When you claim another case is on "all fours" with yours, you are arguing by analogy that because the prior case is similar to yours in all essential respects, the same result should follow. You are using analogical reasoning when you cite a prior decision involving similar facts and, even if not on "all fours," suggest that it may be sufficiently alike in important respects that it compels a like result in the pending dispute. The doctrine of *stare decisis*, by requiring that like cases be decided alike, makes analogical reasoning the foundation of most judicial decision-making. It is analogical reasoning that has been used in the incremental development of the common law. It is also analogical reasoning that the U.S. Supreme Court uses in deciding constitutional cases by referencing prior cases.

Identify your point of comparison. In developing an argument by analogy, you should first identify a proper base point or precedent—something to which your situation will be compared. For example, if resisting a motion for summary judgment, you would search for a relevant precedent involving denial of a summary judgment motion.

Identify factual similarities and differences. After finding the precedent, you should identify the factual similarities and differences between the precedent and your case. No two cases are precisely alike in every respect.

Assess the relative weight of each comparison. You should assess the relevance and importance of the factual similarities and differences. The more factual similarities there are and the more relevant and important they are, the stronger your analogical argument.

Identify false analogies. When the relevant similarities are few, the argument by analogy is logically weak. If the differences are great, the argument may be so weak that it is akin, as the saying goes, to comparing "apples and oranges." When an analogy lacks genuine similarities of relevant characteristics or involves material differences, it is said to be a "false analogy," a type of logical fallacy.

Use a figurative analogy to illustrate your point. Whereas a literal analogy involves a comparison between like cases or classes, a figurative analogy focuses on comparisons between unlike categories. For example, in a trial involving circumstantial evidence, you might weave into your argument Daniel Defoe's story about Robinson Crusoe, who was washed up on an island he thought he alone inhabited. He awoke one morning to find a human footprint in the sand—proving that someone else was on the island just as convincingly as if that person had been standing there in plain sight. As you review the circumstantial facts of your case, you might compare them to the Crusoe story by saying: "Although there is no direct evidence that the defendant was speeding, as Dr. Jones testified, the average time for the trip from the store to the intersection was four minutes. You know that the defendant drove it in two minutes. Like the footprint in the sand, you have solid proof. The defendant was speeding."

Be aware that figurative analogies do not have the force of logic. Figurative analogies, like metaphors, are a useful rhetorical device despite the fact that they do not have the force of logic. [*See* Secret 9, Argue with Style.] They can be helpful in illustrating ideas, particularly abstract ideas, and can be extremely effective in persuasion. Nevertheless, they do not have the same logical power as a literal analogy in which the comparison is between cases that are alike in relevant characteristics. If you are making a legal argument, you are usually better off arguing from a precedent that is on "all fours" than one that is only figuratively relevant.

Use Causal Correlation to Prove Cause or Effect

Identify facts from which a causal inference can be drawn. Inductive reasoning is routinely used to identify and prove the causes of events. If a group of people become ill with food poisoning after eating at a restaurant, and clam chowder was the only food eaten in common by those who got sick, then one can reasonably infer that the clam chowder was the cause of the food poisoning. If the size of the security force at a shopping mall is increased from time to time, and each time the force is increased the number of crimes at the mall proportionally decreases, then one can reasonably infer that the increase in security caused a decrease in crime. In each of these examples, the facts indicate a causal correlation.

Remember that chronology does not prove causation. The mere existence of a correlation in time between two events does not establish a causal relation. When your opponent infers causation merely because one event followed chronologically after another, he has committed what is known as the false cause or *post hoc* fallacy. The latter name comes from the Latin phrase, "*post hoc ergo propter hoc*," which means "after this, therefore, because of this." In 1956, off the shore of Nantucket, a passenger aboard the *Andrea Doria* retired to her cabin. She flicked a light switch and immediately heard a loud crash as the *Andrea Doria* collided with the Stockholm. The lady passenger burst from her cabin and reported to the first person in sight that she must have activated the ship's emergency brake. By assuming that flicking the light switch had caused the loud crash that followed, the lady committed the *post hoc* fallacy.[2] To avoid making the same mistake, ensure that whenever you argue a causal correlation, there is more to indicate a cause-and-effect relationship than merely a suggestive time sequence.

Use Deductive Reasoning to Reach a Conclusion That Is Certain

Start with a general premise. Deductive reasoning often starts with a general premise and reasons to a specific conclusion. For example, if you start with the general premise that all lawsuits for personal injury are barred unless filed within three years of the injury, and it is established that the John Jones lawsuit was filed four years after his injury, you may specifically conclude that John Jones's lawsuit is barred.

Understand the traditional syllogism. The traditional form of deductive argument is the syllogism. A syllogism consists of three parts: a first statement, called the "major premise," a second statement, called the "minor premise," and a "conclusion." The classic example of a syllogism is the following:

Major Premise:	All men are mortal.
Minor Premise:	Socrates is a man.
Conclusion:	Therefore, Socrates is mortal.

Note the two hallmarks of deductive reasoning in this example: the conclusion follows necessarily from the premises, and the conclusion contains no new information. Note also that if the premises are true, the conclusion is not merely probable, it is certain.

Test the truth of the premise. A categorical syllogism affirms that what is true of a class is true of a member of the class. The above example illustrates a categorical syllogism because the major premise makes a statement about a general category or class—in the example, "all men." The minor premise then places a specific person or object within the general category or class. A valid syllogism is not necessarily true. When a syllogism is stated in the correct form, it is said to be "valid," which means that the conclusion logically follows from the premises. Note that there is a significant distinction between validity and truth. Consider this example of categorical syllogism:

Major Premise:	All moons are made of green cheese.
Minor Premise:	Io is a moon of Jupiter.
Conclusion:	Therefore, Io is made of green cheese.

This argument is perfectly valid. The conclusion logically follows from the premises, but it is not true. If one of the premises of a deductive argument is untrue (e.g., "All moons are made of green cheese"), there can be no assurance that the conclusion will be true. If a syllogism is stated in proper form, its conclusion will always be valid, but whether it is true will depend on the truth of the premises. When one of the premises is not true, the arguer has committed the fallacy of "false premise."

Use hypothetical syllogism to resolve uncertainty in the premise. The hypothetical syllogism usually takes the form of "If this, then that." For example:

Major Premise:	If Sam drove the getaway car, then he would be guilty as an accessory.
Minor Premise:	Sam drove the getaway car.
Conclusion:	Therefore, Sam is guilty as an accessory.

In a hypothetical syllogism, the major premise refers to something that is uncertain, and the minor premise affirms or denies whether what was uncertain did occur.

Use disjunctive syllogism to choose between two possible conclusions. A disjunctive syllogism takes the form of an either/or statement, as in the following example:

Major Premise:	Either the insurance company will settle at mediation, or the case will be tried.
Minor Premise:	The insurance company did not settle at mediation.
Conclusion:	Therefore, the case will be tried.

Use Enthymeme When Your Listener Already Believes a Premise

Rely on an accepted premise. Not all premises of deductive arguments need to be proven. Often, premises may be based on the preexisting beliefs of your listener. When you rely on such beliefs for a premise, your deductive argument is referred to as an enthymeme. With an enthymeme, it is not even necessary to state the premise that is already believed. As a practical matter, most deductive arguments in everyday life are of this type. To convince your listener that a witness is smart, you might just say that he is a rocket scientist. Your listener will supply the implicit premise of a belief that rocket scientists are smart. To establish that a car gets poor gas mileage, you might just mention that it has a V-8 engine. Your listener will supply the premise that cars with V-8 engines get poor gas mileage. As long as your listener believes the unproved premise, whether stated or unstated, your enthymeme will be successful as a tool of persuasion.

Assess the truth of the unstated premise. When an enthymeme is used with the premise left unstated, it is important to ascertain this implied premise because it may be the vulnerable point in the argument. Suppose your opponent argues, "The driver smelled of alcohol. So, it's clear he was drunk." This can be analyzed as an enthymeme that relies on the unstated premise that all people who smell of alcohol are drunk. When the premise is made explicit, the weakness of the argument becomes apparent, because someone who has only had one drink may smell of alcohol but not necessarily be drunk. You might consider arguing: "Fred Jenks is a religious man. Therefore, you can believe his testimony." The unstated premise of this enthymeme is that religious men tell the truth. Some listeners will accept this premise; some will not. Before making an argument by enthymeme, you must be sure your listener shares your belief in any unproven premises.

Consider Argument from Definition

Identify the criteria of the definition. As a lawyer, you frequently attempt to convince a judge or jury that a specific person, object, or course of conduct meets a definition that has legal consequences. For example, you may argue that a specific course of conduct created a "contract," a financial instrument qualified as a "security," or a killing was "involuntary manslaughter." In making these arguments, you would look to the law for a definition that identifies the significant criteria and then argue that the circumstances in the case meet these criteria. This is arguing deductively from definition, as in the following example:

Major Premise:	An enforceable contract is created when there is (1) an offer; (2) an acceptance; and (3) consideration.
Minor Premise:	Sam Spade made (1) an offer to Jenny Jarrett that was (2) accepted and (3) supported by consideration.
Conclusion:	Sam Spade and Jenny Jarrett have an enforceable contract.

Use terms consistently. When making an argument from definition, be consistent in your use of terms. Your argument will be valid only if your terms have the same meaning throughout. If the term "consideration" used in the above example in the major premise meant something of value given in exchange but in the minor premise referred to Sam's sympathetic regard for Jenny, then the argument would be a fallacy or an "equivocation," which occurs when the same term is used with two or more distinct meanings.

Learn to Spot Fallacies and Weaknesses in Arguments

Fallacies discussed so far in this chapter relate to particular types of logical arguments that include hasty generalization, failure to account for negative instances, false analogy, *post hoc* (false cause), false premise, and equivocation. Other types of fallacies may occur in any type of argument, and you will frequently encounter them in the practice of law. It is therefore wise to watch for erroneous reasoning whenever you engage in argument. Even if you cannot label an argument as a particular kind of fallacy, you should still be able to tell by careful analysis whether the reasons given are sound and whether the conclusion logically follows. This careful analysis in search of faulty reasoning is a critical step in building a powerful argument to support your position and counter the argument of your opponent. The following constitute some of the most commonly occurring fallacies.

BEGGING THE QUESTION

Be alert to "reasons" that simply restate the claim. Begging the question occurs when the argument assumes the conclusion in a premise of the argument and results in circular reasoning.

An example is the following exchange between comedians George Burns and Gracie Allen:

GRACIE: Gentlemen prefer blondes.
GEORGE: How do you know that?
GRACIE: A gentleman told me so.
GEORGE: How did you know he was a gentleman?
GRACIE: Because he preferred blondes.

Circular reasoning in a legal argument is rarely as obvious as this example. Usually, the fallacy occurs when a claim is supported by a reason that uses different words but amounts to no more than a restatement of the claim. Consider, for example, the argument "Abortion is murder because it involves the intentional killing of an unborn human being." Murder is by definition the intentional killing of another human being. The critical issue in the abortion debate is not whether there has been an intentional killing but whether the fetus is a human being under the law. The example, by assuming that the fetus is a human being, avoids the critical issue, begging the question whether the fetus is a human being, and makes a circular argument. Judge Learned Hand observed that "no other single fault has done more to confuse the law and to disseminate litigation" than the fallacy of begging the question.[3] In fact, Hand believed that with respect to this fallacy, "We are all sinners; nobody's record is clean." In light of its prevalence, you should always be on the lookout for instances of circular reasoning in your own arguments as well as those of your opponents.

AD HOMINEM

Address argument to issues, not people. "*Ad hominem*" means "to the man or person," and such an argument occurs when an advocate makes a personal attack on the opponent, not the substance of the opponent's argument. You may have heard the advice, usually given with tongue firmly planted in cheek, "If the law is against you, argue the facts. If the facts are against you, argue to the law. And if the facts and the law are both against you, abuse your adversary." An advocate who resorts to abusing his adversary commits the *ad hominem* fallacy. Ideally, arguments should be "*ad rem*," meaning "to the thing"—the argument should be addressed to the issues in dispute, not to the character of the opposing advocate.

Avoid name-calling. In its crudest form, the *ad hominem* argument involves nothing more than name-calling. Our vocabulary offers a rich array of choices to deride an opponent, such as idiot, low-life, airhead, bleeding heart, wimp, and the like. In one reported case, an irate attorney characterized his opponent on the record as "dense, a culprit so lacking in mental capacity as not able to find his way to the toilet, too big for his britches, a skunk, a jack-leg, lazy, tricky, unfit to practice law," and a "son of a bitch."[4] Such attacks constitute a logical fallacy and could even be grounds for disbarment, as this irate lawyer later learned to his dismay.

Attack the credibility of your opponent's authority. Not all attacks on the person are fallacious. When an opponent relies on an expert to support a proposition, it is not fallacious to attack the credibility of the alleged expert. The bias, dishonesty, and lack of expertise of a proffered authority are all fair game and logically serve to undermine the opponent's reliance on the purported expert. Nevertheless, it should be understood that such argument, since it is directed to the person, does not prove or disprove the merits of the case; its impact is limited to negating an opposing argument relying on that authority.

RED HERRING

Counter attempts to distract your listener with irrelevancies. The "red herring" fallacy is committed when an advocate focuses on a false, irrelevant, or minor issue to distract attention from the principal issues. The term "red herring" arose as a hunting term in the 1600s when a red herring (a type of smelly fish) was drawn across the

Avoid Deriding Your Opponent's Conduct or Feelings

A more subtle form of the *ad hominem* argument is to attack in a derisive way the opponent's conduct or feelings. In argument to a jury in a criminal case, a prosecutor stated, "Counsel for the defendant are trying to make monkeys out of this jury, and they are laughing up their sleeves at you."[5] Comments like this do not advance an argument on the merits but are intended, by attacking the opponent, to bias your listener against the substance of the opponent's argument. Such technique is not only a logical fallacy but in extreme circumstances might lead to reversal of a favorable verdict on grounds of improper argument. In fact, that is exactly what happened in the above example.

path of a fox to throw the hounds off the fox's scent. Similarly, an advocate whose arguments on the merits are weak may try to distract the decision-maker by focusing on false, irrelevant, or minor issues. An effective response to such an argument is to identify the tactic for what it is—a distraction, like a red herring. For example, when a criminal defense lawyer attempts to focus attention on whether the government should have granted immunity to a witness, the prosecutor should point out that "the real issue is whether the defendant committed the crime. The issue of immunity is just a red herring."

STRAW MAN

Counter distortions of your argument. The "straw man" fallacy occurs when an advocate describes an opponent's position in an oversimplified or extreme form and then refutes this distortion of the opponent's position instead of addressing the opponent's real position. By setting up a straw man that can be blown away, the advocate creates the misleading impression that he has destroyed the opposing argument, when, in fact, he has failed to meet the argument squarely. Usually, a straw man argument can be effectively countered simply by identifying it as a distortion. Sometimes, though, particularly when there is no opportunity for the opposition to respond, a straw man argument may succeed. Richard Nixon used this tactic during his 1952 vice-presidential campaign in the "Checkers Speech," in which Nixon responded to accusations that he had improperly appropriated $18,000 in campaign funds for his personal use. Instead of responding directly to accusations involving the money, Nixon talked about another gift that he had received during the campaign from a supporter in Texas:

It was a little cocker spaniel dog, in a crate that he had sent all the way from Texas, black and white, spotted, and our little girl, Tricia, the six-year-old, named it Checkers. And, you know, the kids, like all kids, loved the dog, and I just want to say this, right now, that regardless of what they say about it, we are going to keep it.

Of course, Nixon's accusers had never suggested that his daughters be deprived of their beloved dog. It was a straw man argument that, although fallacious, proved to be politically effective.

SLIPPERY SLOPE

Test for safe stopping places. The "slippery slope" argument falsely assumes that once you take a moderate first step in a particular direction, a catastrophic chain of events will follow. Gun control opponents argue against limits on the sale of automatic assault weapons because confiscation of sportsmen's shotguns will soon follow. Bureaucrats defend their unbending enforcement of a regulation, even in circumstances that are patently unfair, because allowing an exception would "open the floodgates." These types of arguments are fallacious because they falsely describe the slope as slippery when the reality is more like a staircase with many safe stopping places along the way. In the gun control example, the government could prohibit some types of particularly dangerous weapons without taking the further step of outlawing shotguns. Bureaucrats facing enforcement regulations could create a narrow exception to a rule when warranted without affecting all other situations. On the other hand, sometimes the slope is truly slippery, and acceptance of a particular position can lead to a catastrophic chain of events. In such situations, the slippery slope argument is a legitimate basis of argument.

COMPOUND QUESTIONS

Identify compound questions that assume a false premise. The compound question fallacy occurs when an argument is phrased as a single question seeking a single answer but actually involves two or more issues that cannot be answered accurately with a single response. The classic example is the question "Have you stopped beating your wife?" The first issue is whether you have ever beaten your wife, the second, whether you have stopped. The question cannot be correctly answered with a simple yes or no if you never previously beat your wife. Usually, your best response to such a question is to point out that the questioner has made a false or unwarranted assumption. Consider the question "Are you still sexually harassing the staff?" An appropriate response would be: "The question presumes that I have sexually harassed the staff in the past. That is a false presumption. Since your question is based on a false presumption, it cannot be correctly answered as phrased." Do not confuse the compound question fallacy with the evidentiary objection for compound questions. For evidentiary purposes, any question that asks several things at once may be objectionable on grounds that it is compound. The concern of the objection is that the question may confuse the witness or the jury. A fallacy is not necessarily involved.

FALSE DILEMMA

Search for all possible alternatives before attacking on grounds of dilemma. Closely related to the compound question fallacy is the fallacy of the false dilemma or false dichotomy. The compound question wrongly suggests that there is only a single answer to a question that poses more than one issue. The false dilemma wrongly suggests that there are only two alternatives when there are actually many. It may be argued that a witness is either telling the truth or lying, and that because what he said was proved to be false, he must have lied. On the other hand, lying—the intentional telling of a falsehood—may not be the only alternative to telling the truth. A witness may have unintentionally uttered a falsehood due to poor memory, confusion, miscommunication, or the like. Situations are often more complex than the either/or premise an advocate may use to try to box in an opponent. On the other hand, there are times when there are only two choices, neither of which is desirable. It may be that the defendant was either driving too fast to react or, if driving slower, was not paying proper attention. Such circumstances can provide the basis for a powerful argument. Make sure that these are the only choices. If you seek to place your opponent on the horns of a dilemma, you may find yourself impaled by your own argument when a third reasonable alternative is discovered.

COMPOSITION AND DIVISION

Test whether what is true of the whole is also true of the parts. The fallacy of division is the mirror image of the fallacy of composition: it assumes that what is true of the whole is true of the collective parts. Just as it is erroneous to assume that players of average talent will be an average team, so also is it erroneous to infer the reverse—

Test Whether What Is True of the Parts Is Also True of the Whole

The fallacy of composition assumes that what is true of the separate parts is necessarily true of the collective whole. If you employ three excellent lawyers to defend a case, you may wrongly assume that they will be an excellent legal team. They may not be a great team if they have conflicting views of the case or conflicting styles, or if they all want to be in charge. Instead of a "dream team," you may have a nightmare. Alternatively, a collective whole may be more than the sum of its parts. A group of basketball players with only average talent may, with good coaching and unselfish play, become an excellent team. It is logically unsound to infer that what is true of the parts must be true of the whole.

that an excellent team must consist of excellent players. What is true of a class may not be true of individual members of a class.

NON SEQUITUR

Identify gaps in the reasoning chain. The term "*non sequitur*" means "it does not follow" and refers to a claim that does not logically follow from the stated premises. In one sense, all logical fallacies are *non sequiturs*, but the label is ordinarily used in only three situations, all of which involve an erroneous or missing link. The first is an argument that involves a completely illogical leap or assumes a false premise: "The witness should not be believed because he smokes cigars." This argument assumes that all persons who smoke cigars cannot be believed. There is no logical connection between smoking cigars and credibility; therefore, the argument is a *non sequitur*. The second occurs when there is a missing premise: "People who wear nose rings are disgusting. There ought to be a law against wearing nose rings in public." The gap in this reasoning is the absence of the premise, "There ought to be a law against anything I find disgusting." The third involves irrelevant reasons used to support a claim: "I should get a salary increase this year because I received a raise last year." A person's performance and value to the employer justify a salary hike, not whether a raise was previously received. The argument avoids being a *non sequitur* if it contains additional information such as "My performance this year was better than last year."

NOTES

1. Benjamin N. Cardozo, *The Nature of the Judicial Process* pp. 22–23 (1921) (Reprint 1985, Yale University Press).
2. Ruggero J. Aldisert, *Logic for Lawyers: A Guide to Clear Legal Thinking* p. 194 (1989).
3. Thomas Walter Swan, "Hand," 57 *Yale L.J.* 107, 170 (1947).
4. *In the Matter of Crumpacker*, 383 N.E.2d 36, 49 (Ind. 1978), *cert. denied*, 444 U.S. 979 (1979).
5. *Crook v. Alabama*, 42 Ala. App. 270, 160 So. 2d 884, 886–87 (1963).

Secret 5 Build with Evidence, Law, and Policy

The foundation of your argument, on which everything else is built, is substance. Sometimes substance is apparent; often, however, you have the opportunity to be creative. To craft a persuasive argument, you need to find ways to develop the substance that will support your legal and factual theories and themes.

Develop Your Substantive Case

Understand that substance matters most. Although many factors can influence whether an argument will succeed or fail, almost always, what matters most will be the evidence, the law, and other substantive content that supports your client's position. Louis Nizer was correct when he observed, "Juries decide issues on fact." In other words, "you win cases because you have established the facts in your favor."[1] Similarly, when judges are the decision-makers, you win cases when you establish that the law is in your favor. Were it otherwise, our system of justice could be criticized, and rightly so, for resolving cases based not on the merits but rather on who had the best lawyer. In our experience, most verdicts by both judges and juries are decided on the merits. As a result, truth and justice generally prevail.

Take responsibility for the development of your case. As a lawyer, you have three important responsibilities for the development of the substantive content of your argument. First, you find and gather the content. This will include the pertinent facts, relevant law, and any other materials that might have value in your argument. Second, you evaluate what you collected and select the most helpful content. Third, you design and build a persuasive argument out of materials you selected.

Be Creative in Building Your Best Case

Understand the continued vitality of the classical concept of invention. In Cicero's time, "invention" was considered the most important component of persuasion. Used in this context, invention means the development and selection of the material or the line of argument that makes a case convincing.[2] The concept is as old as Plato and was discussed thoroughly by Aristotle.[3] The primary challenge of invention is one of identification: to identify the ideas and framework by which the hard facts and other content are made most persuasive. In classical oratory, when speakers were searching for material around which to develop an argument, they turned to a well-known list of topics. On this list were ideas like honor, patriotism, laws, and the relationships between things. The list was designed, at least in part, to spark thinking "outside the box" of the particular case and thereby to inspire other lines of argument. Though the list remains a workable starting place, its value is in its symbolic reminder that creativity and invention have a very real place in the construction of effective argument.

Use your imagination to create something new and original. Sir Walter Scott observed that in collecting, evaluating, and selecting the most useful material, the lawyer's work is like that of a mason who gathers and selects the most appropriate stones for construction. But the best lawyers, according to Scott, are less like masons and more like architects, using knowledge, thought, and creativity to design new and original buildings. When you practice your art at its highest level, you use the raw materials—the facts and the law—to create something new, original, and sturdy: a convincing argument.

Think outside the box. As a lawyer, you routinely address certain issues, including the legal elements of the case, the defenses offered, the credibility of witnesses, and the burden of proof—all appropriate and necessary concerns. Nevertheless, if you want to make the strongest argument possible, you must look beyond the obvious to identify other issues or values that may be at stake. For example, when you argue in a breach of contract case, you might talk simply in terms of "strict enforcement of agreed terms." Alternatively, you might cradle your facts in themes, such as "honoring commitments" or "fulfilling corporate responsibilities." Below are two good examples of thinking outside the box in legal argument.

Turn a problem into a strength. In the *Leopold and Loeb* case, the media regularly reported that the wealthy families of the defendants had been able to hire the best legal counsel and would receive special treatment from the courts. In his closing argument, Clarence Darrow turned this problem into a strength. He argued against the imposition of the death penalty in this way:

> *If we fail in this defense, it will not be for lack of money. It will be on account of money. Money has been the most serious handicap that we have met. There are times when poverty is fortunate.*
>
> *I insist, your Honor, that had this been the case of these defendants' age, unconnected with families supposed to have great wealth, there is not a State's Attorney in Illinois who would not have consented at once to a plea of guilty and punishment in the penitentiary for life. No one . . .* [4]

Consider Undertaking a Burden of Proof Not Legally Yours

Another example of creative thinking is undertaking a burden that is not legally yours. Thus, as counsel for the defense in a civil or criminal case, you might decide to tell the jury directly what the defense will prove, rather than pointing out to the jury that the burden of proof belongs to the plaintiff or to the prosecution. For example: "Ladies and gentlemen of the jury, we are going to *prove* to you that Mr. Smith is innocent." This is consistent with the advice offered by famed attorney Herbert Stern, who advises, "Never defend any case. All cases must be prosecuted."[5] Of course, whether the best defense is a good offense will be for you to judge in your own particular case, but it is an example of out-of-the box thinking that you should consider.

Thoroughly Research Your Argument

Search for all relevant material. Before presenting an argument on any matter, it is essential that you conduct a thorough search for all potentially relevant material. If the issue is a factual one, then you must carefully investigate the pertinent facts. In litigation, this is typically done through interrogatories, requests for production of documents, depositions, witness interviews, examination of the accident scene, and the like. If the issue is one of law, then you must find all the relevant law, such as cases, statutes, treaties and regulations.

Brainstorm to identify all potential sources of information. For many kinds of arguments, there are usual and customary sources of relevant information. For example, in an automobile accident case, you would routinely obtain the police accident report, the plaintiff's medical records, photos of the accident scene, and statements of witnesses. Do not, however, limit yourself to these routine materials. There may be additional sources of helpful information like a report if the fire department was called to the scene, social security records if the plaintiff filed for disability, or employment records if the plaintiff is claiming lost time. The internet has become a rich source of relevant data. And don't forget the old cliché: two heads are better than one. As you begin the process of preparing an argument, consider brainstorming with colleagues for ideas about where additional information might be located. There are, of course, practical limits on how far you can search, but do not start the process with blinders on. Sometimes the most powerful information can be found in unexpected places.

Use information as the ammunition of argument. In war, the side with the best ammunition usually wins. In argument, the side with best information usually wins. Therefore, as you prepare to argue, make sure that you have gathered all of the available relevant information, wherever it may be found.

Develop Your Theory of the Case

Determine the fundamental reason why you should win. After you have gathered the relevant information, you must analyze it. During this analysis, identify the fundamental reason why you should win the argument. Express that reason in its simplest terms. This fundamental reason, simply expressed, is the theory of your argument. Sometimes the theory will be obvious. Other times hard thinking will be required, with many possibilities considered and rejected before you settle on the theory that is most promising.

Derive your theory from legal principles. In a breach of contract case, the defendant's theory might be that there is no contract because there was no meeting of the minds. In an employment discrimination suit, the plaintiff's theory might be that by ignoring the lewd jokes, comments, and internal correspondence that permeated the workplace, the defendant allowed the creation of a hostile work environment. In a bribery case, the defendant's theory might be that the item received was too insignificant to have affected the recipient's actions. Deciding on a theory requires distilling the mass of relevant facts and law in the case to identify the issue that is most likely to yield a favorable result for your client. Your theory is the basis of your argument. Thus, as you set about to formulate your argument, make sure that you can clearly articulate the legal theory by which your client prevails.

Select Key Persuasive Points as Themes

Ground themes in shared human experiences. As you analyze the material that you have gathered for your argument, develop short, fact-based statements of why persuasively—rather than legally—your client should prevail. These will be the themes of your case. The best themes are grounded in common sense and shared human experiences such as fairness and honor and should resonate emotionally with your listener. [*See* Secret 6, Appeal to Emotion.]

Use themes consistent with your listeners' beliefs. Like others seeking to make sense of new information, jurors use an analytical (generally deductive) framework to evaluate the evidence in a case. The jurors take a general proposition (something familiar) and reason to a specific conclusion (something new and potentially unfamiliar). The more familiar the route, the easier the travel. Thus, the more your theme provides a contextual roadmap for this reasoning process, the more you are likely to succeed. In this context, using something "familiar" does not mean that you should resist thinking outside the box or that you should abandon creative or innovative themes that can bring elements of surprise and pleasure to your argument. This is about how you ask the decision-maker to reason and does, therefore, mean that you should avoid cognitive dissonance.

For example, most people believe that parents seek to protect their children. A theme that most parents would save themselves at the expense of a child is an example of a theme replete with cognitive dissonance. It is possible of course that the parents in your case indeed sacrificed their child for their own well-being, but the notion rubs at the core of our beliefs and tends to make us skeptical. If you want the decision-maker to believe that the parents in your case sacrificed their own child for their own well-being, you should find a theme that seeks to explain their decision in a way that the decision-maker would understand, such as callous greed or sexual extremism.

Respect the importance of evaluative context. In developing your theme, keep in mind two last points. First, in some situations your listener's evaluative context may matter more than science or other evidence. For example, in the trial of a person accused of destroying a building where abortions are performed, jurors' views regarding contraception and issues of self-determination may mean as much as the physical evidence linking the defendant to the scene. Second, if you fail to provide an appropriate evaluative context, your jurors will develop and employ their own.[6]

Employ memorable themes. A theme should be short, pithy, partisan, and memorable. You want your listener to repeat the theme when she is considering her decision. If she repeats "This is David taking on Goliath" or "When you try to cut corners, things get lost," the theme starts to provide an evaluative context, by providing the setting from which your listener sets out to resolve the issues.

Review the Key Facts to Find Potential Themes

How do you select a theme? Sometimes one will jump out at you. Where that does not happen, try this technique. Once you have settled on your legal theory, make a list of the important facts that support that theory. Include only facts the jury is likely to believe. From this list, try to find patterns or commonalities that suggest a theme. Alternatively, you might focus on one fact that is central to your argument and express that key fact in a memorable way.

In this way, a theme is like a silent ally in the decision-making process—the equivalent of a small voice whispering in your listener's ear, repeatedly restating the context of the deliberations. In jury deliberations, this can be particularly effective. If you can get one or more jurors repeating your theme, it is as if you are a participant in the deliberations—every advocate's secret dream.

Make sure facts and themes are consistent. You would be amazed at the number of cases in which lawyers present a series of facts that, when considered collectively, do not hang together. Get in the habit of saying to yourself: "This is what I believed happened. And if X happened, then Y must be true." Does Y appear to be true? If not, stop and rethink your factual explanation. Then continue: "If X happened, Z cannot be true." Does it appear as though Z is true? If so, stop and reconsider. By way of example, imagine that through discovery plaintiff's counsel finds information suggesting that the defendant company's business decisions were motivated by a desire to take over a competitor. Elsewhere, plaintiff's counsel finds evidence suggesting that the defendant's actions were motivated by lack of interest in continuing in a particular line of business. It is possible that both motivations are true, but it is unlikely. The plaintiff should ask, "Which is the more likely explanation for what happened?" Unless the plaintiff can answer this question, it will be difficult for your listener to do so. It is possible that evidence of declining interest was fabricated in order to mislead anyone who may have suspected the takeover efforts. The facts, then, might be cast as follows: "This is a company concerned only with pursuing its own agenda, with no respect for truth or for honoring its commitments." To develop a theme, first identify what you think happened. Then reduce the events to a short, memorable expression that accords with people's common experience and grabs us emotionally.

Recognize Theories and Themes in Arguments of Others

Your skill in developing and using theories and themes in your own arguments will be enhanced if you are alert to these elements in arguments presented by others. When listening to or reading an argument, ask yourself, "What was the theory of the argument? What themes were employed?" This exercise can be helpful not only in court but when reading an argument in a book or watching one in a movie. For example, in Shakespeare's *Julius Caesar*, Brutus makes a public speech to an audience of Romans to persuade them that he was justified in slaying Caesar. At the beginning of this speech, Brutus introduces the theory of his argument and his principal theme:

Romans, countrymen, and lovers!

Hear me for my cause, and be silent, that you may hear: believe me for mine honor, and have respect to mine honor, that you may believe: censure me in your wisdom, and awake your senses, that you may be the better judge. If there be any in this assembly, any dear friend of Caesar's, to him I say, that Brutus' love to Caesar was no less than his. If then that friend demand why Brutus rose against Caesar, this is my answer: Not that I loved Caesar less, but that I loved Rome more. Had you rather Caesar were living and die all slaves, than that Caesar were dead, to live all free men? As Caesar loved me, I weep for him; as he was fortunate,

I rejoice at it; as he was valiant, I honor him; but, as he was ambitious, I slew him. There are tears for his love; joy for his fortune; honor for his valor; and death for his ambition. Who is here so base that would be a bondsman? If any speak; for him have I offended. Who is here so rude that he would not be a Roman? If any, speak; for him have I offended. I pause for a reply.[7]

The fundamental reason propounded by Brutus for slaying Caesar was that, given Caesar's ambition, if he had not been slain, all Romans would have become slaves. This is the theory of his argument. A theme used to support the argument was Brutus's love for Rome, expressed memorably in the line "Not that I loved Caesar less, but that I loved Rome more." Although this example represents a style not compatible with modern elocution, it nonetheless provides a compelling example of an argument that, in short order, successfully establishes the advocate's theory and theme.

Emphasize Your Theme

Introduce your theme early and often. Introduce your theme early in the case, and repeat it often.[8] Deftly used, a theme can take on the characteristics of a conditioned emotional response (like Pavlov's dog). If the plaintiff associates the defendant with corporate greed often enough, or the defendant associates the plaintiff with irresponsibility often enough, the conditioned association may become automatic and may happen without much, if any, cognitive activity on the part of the jurors.[9]

Reinforce your theme in varied ways. Reinforce your theme by using variety in detail and wording. If your theme in defending an antitrust case is that the plaintiff has an inflated view of its market share, instead of repeatedly using the word "inflated," consider other words that reinforce the nonscientific nature of the plaintiff's evidence—words such as "estimated," "approximate," "projected," "gauge," and "theorize." Avoid using words like "calculate" and "compute" because they connote precision.

Beware of theme overuse. One author reports that, after a lengthy trial, "Jurors disclosed that they were tired of hearing the same theme repeated by one side's witnesses. Whenever the words 'risk of harm' were uttered, one juror sitting in the front row, whose hands were hidden below the front wall of the jury box, waved her hands like a conductor whenever the same old tune appeared."[10]

You can certainly guess that the theme-prone lawyer did not know of this phenomenon until long after the verdict was returned. It is a lesson, nevertheless, from which you can benefit. Similarly, repeated use of a thematic phrase by your witnesses can sound orchestrated and insincere. Tout your theme early, communicate it clearly, but do not repeat it so often that it becomes cliché.

Select the Most Helpful Information

Consider all relevant information. A key step in the preparation of your argument is the selection of the information on which you will rely. This selection process requires consideration of all of the relevant information that was gathered and is guided by your theory of the case and the themes that you developed. In evaluating the available information, there are many factors to consider that will vary depending on the issues involved.

On issues of fact, consider the weight of the evidence. When the issue in dispute is a factual one, the evidence will provide the crucial content for your argument. In evaluating which evidence to include in your argument, your principal concern will be its persuasive value or weight. When you studied evidence in law school, your primary focus was on the question of admissibility. In considering admissibility, it is common to note that a particular concern may negatively affect the weight of the evidence, but not its admissibility. In evaluating evidence for use in argument, it is the weight of the evidence that matters.[11]

On Issues of Law, Apply Standard Legal Criteria

When the issue is purely legal in nature, the information that you will evaluate will consist primarily of the same kind of material that you routinely studied in law school: appellate court decisions, statutes, treaties, rules, and regulations. For example, in evaluating which cases to cite to a trial judge on a motion to dismiss, you would consider the following: Is the case on point? Is it authored by a court that the trial judge is compelled to follow, e.g., the state supreme court? Is it recent or ancient? Is it well-reasoned? Is the pertinent discussion a holding or mere dictum? Have subsequent cases supported or discredited the court's holding? If the legal issue is one of first impression in the jurisdiction, the most important information may relate to public policy considerations. If the legal issue concerns statutory construction, the critical information may be found in the legislative history.

Don't ignore inadmissible evidence. The weight of a particular piece of evidence will ordinarily be affected by specific circumstances far too numerous and varied to be addressed here. Remember that for purposes of argument outside the trial context, evidence may encompass more than the material that would be admissible in court. In this broader sense, evidence includes any facts, data, or opinions that are used to support a claim. So in negotiating a settlement, for example, you might cite a jury verdict of $250,000 in a similar case to support your assessment of the value of the case. Although not admissible at trial, the result in the similar case is nonetheless relevant and probative "evidence" of settlement value for purposes of your argument in the negotiation. Thus, when you think of evidence for purposes of argument, do not limit your consideration only to what is admissible under the law of evidence.

Evaluate Evidence in Relation to the Audience

Differentiate first-, second-, and third-order data. One way of analyzing the weight of evidence is in relation to the audience. If the audience already believes a fact—for example, if they have seen it with their own eyes—it is referred to as first-order data, the highest category. When O. J. Simpson tried on the bloody glove and the jury saw that it did not fit, that fact became the most persuasive in the trial. Second-order data include facts and opinions asserted by the speaker and are, accordingly, dependent on the credibility of the speaker. Third-order data are facts and opinions to which a speaker may refer but which are attributed to others. The persuasiveness of third-order data depends on the credibility of the outside informant as well as on the credibility of the speaker. Not surprisingly, it is usually less persuasive than first or second-order data.

Give priority to first-order data. In considering the quality of evidence, first-order data is most persuasive—things the audience already believes or can see with their own eyes. There's an old Russian saying: "It is better to see something once than to hear about it a hundred times." Thus, showing the jury firsthand how the plaintiff struggles to walk in a body cast is more powerful than witness testimony to that effect.

Use second-order data when first-order data is not available. A fact testified to by a witness is second-order data. Second-order data is almost always stronger than a statement by an advocate about what the witness said.

Augment third-order data. Third-order data is in essence hearsay. When you argue in a pretrial mediation that a witness will testify to a particular fact, acceptance of your argument will depend both on what your listener thinks of you and what she thinks of the witness. Because third-order data are the weakest, at least conceptually, you will be more persuasive if you can corroborate the data. This means, for example, that in the negotiation argument referred to above, instead of just telling your adversary about the $250,000 verdict, give him a copy of the published case so he can see the results for himself.

Use the Most Persuasive Evidence: Direct, Circumstantial, or Real

Distinguish between direct and circumstantial evidence. In his classic treatise on the law of evidence, Wigmore identified three basic types of evidence: direct evidence, circumstantial, and real.[12] When a witness testifies "I saw the defendant at the murder scene," she is providing direct evidence of that fact. Circumstantial evidence, on the other hand, requires your listener to draw an inference; additional reasoning is required. Proof that the defendant's handkerchief was found at the murder scene constitutes circumstantial evidence that the defendant was there. It does not prove the point directly but relies on an inference. An inference from circumstantial evidence may be strong or weak, true or false. Direct evidence has one distinct advantage over circumstantial evidence: it requires no inference. Nevertheless, in some situations, circumstantial evidence may be stronger than direct evidence. For example, evidence of the defendant's footprint in the snow under the victim's bedroom window might be more convincing than his wife's testimony that he was at home at the time. In addition, there may be evidence of a number of circumstances that, while not individually convincing, paint a compelling picture of what happened when considered collectively. Contrary to its reputation, a circumstantial case can be as persuasive as the strongest case based on direct evidence. The probative value of circumstantial evidence depends not only on whether the evidence itself is believable but also on the strength of the inference.

When you rely on circumstantial evidence, take the time to explain to your listener how powerful and revealing circumstantial evidence can be. You might want to demonstrate the point with a good example of circumstantial evidence, such as a footprint in the snow. Similarly, when your opponent relies on circumstantial evidence, point out where it is not persuasive. In the example above, that the defendant's handkerchief was found at the murder scene may provide circumstantial evidence that the defendant was there. However, it does not necessarily mean he was there at or near the time of the murder.

Use Real Evidence for Impact

In contrast to direct and circumstantial evidence, real evidence is the thing itself. It is the gun that was used to kill, the ladder from which the plaintiff fell or, as in Irving Younger's legendary illustration, the actual leg that was amputated. If you want to prove something about an object, there is generally no better evidence than the thing itself. There are, however, exceptions to this general rule. For various reasons, the real thing may not make the desired impression. A warning label on the inside of a football helmet may look small and insignificant in real life. Instead of passing the actual helmet to the jury, you may make a greater impact by projecting the warning onto a large screen. Whenever the real thing has warts, literally or figuratively, you might be better off with demonstrative evidence, like a photograph or model of the real thing, that de-emphasizes the warts. Be careful, however, that you do not take such extreme liberties with a substitute for the real thing that your audience thinks you are trying to mislead them.

Weigh Fact versus Opinion Evidence

Determine whether evidence is fact or opinion. In assessing the weight of evidence, an important factor to consider is whether the evidence is a matter of fact or opinion. Proof that the speed recorder on a locomotive read 45 miles per hour at the time of the collision is evidence of a fact. Testimony of an eyewitness standing near the grade crossing at the time of the collision that estimates the train's speed at 70 miles per hour is opinion evidence. Opinions involve interpretations of facts. As a general rule, opinion evidence is not as strong as fact evidence, although there are many exceptions to this rule.

Bolster opinion evidence by establishing credibility and basis. The weight of opinion evidence rests primarily on the credibility of the opinion-giver and the basis for the opinion. When relying on opinion evidence, you will need to present reasons for your audience to accept the opinion as sound. These reasons will vary depending on, among other things, whether the source of the opinion is a layperson or an expert. When an eyewitness offers an opinion on a subject like the speed of a train, the primary concerns are with the witness's ability to observe the train and his experience with estimating speed. When an accident reconstructionist offers an expert opinion on the same issue, the focus shifts to concerns about the qualifications of the witness and the reliability of the methodology employed to arrive at his opinion. Rarely will an expert's opinion be accepted solely on the expert's credentials alone. In the adversarial arenas in which you work, judges and juries want to hear the facts on which the expert's opinion is based. They may not fully comprehend the expert's science, but before accepting the opinion, they will want more of a rationale than just "because the expert said so."[13] Of course, getting expert testimony into evidence now requires that the reliability of the opinion be established.[14]

The acquisition, retention, retrieval, and communication of evidence affects its persuasive value. If fact evidence is provided by witness testimony, its strength will be affected by the witness's ability to acquire, retain, retrieve, and communicate the pertinent information.

Acquisition. A witness's ability to acquire information may be affected by a wide variety of circumstances. These include acuity of the witness's eyesight, lighting in the area, distance from the witness to the object of concern, length of time available to make the observation, influence of alcohol or other drugs that the witness may have consumed, obstructions that were between the witness and the object, distractions at the scene, and alertness of the witness.

Retention and Retrieval. Even if information is adequately acquired, the witness's ability to retain and retrieve it may be influenced by several factors. These include the quality of the witness's memory in general, time elapsed since the event, impression made by the initial perception, statements by others about what happened, and events in the witness's life since the observation such as health problems or observations of similar events or objects.

Communication. Even witnesses who successfully acquire, retain, and retrieve information may still encounter difficulties in communicating it. Some witnesses have limited vocabularies. Due to nervousness, the witness may find himself tongue-tied. If English is not the witness's native language, her accent may impair the listener's understanding. Some witnesses are simply unable to express themselves clearly.

All of the above factors can influence the weight given to witness evidence and should be considered when relying on it in argument.[15]

Determine the existence of bias. Whether a witness is an expert or layperson, a primary consideration in evaluating the witness's credibility is bias. If a witness has a motive to be anything other than objective, that motive will affect the persuasive weight of the witness's testimony. Bias can result from many factors: the witness is a friend, relative, or employee of a party in interest; the witness will be paid for the testimony, in cash or in immunity from prosecution; or the witness has some other motive to color his testimony to favor or oppose a party. For all evidence used in an argument, you should investigate whether the source of that evidence is biased. As a general rule, give more emphasis to helpful evidence from an unbiased source, such as a disinterested bystander, than to witnesses who are vulnerable to attack on grounds of bias.

Use Statistical Evidence Effectively

Assess the validity of statistics. Statistics are a type of evidence in which information is expressed through numbers. Statistics can be extremely persuasive. They can also be used to mislead. In evaluating statistical evidence for use in argument, it is helpful to consider a few general questions:

Are the statistics based on a representative sample? Statistics are usually just a quantified form of examples. Like other examples, to be valid they need to be representative of the entire population, class of items, or events. To be representative, a sample must be randomly selected. For example, a selection is random if every person in the population had an equal chance of being included. You cannot gauge a community's attitude toward a proposed liquor tax by polling only the citizens at a corner tavern or members of a neighboring fundamentalist church.

Are the units of comparison equal? The items being compared should be expressed in the same statistical units. If not, the data will be misleading. You cannot compare demand for Starbucks coffee if one store counts cups that are used and another counts cash register records. The former doesn't account for wasted cups and the latter doesn't account for free coffee.

Is the source reliable? Statistics, like any other kind of evidence, are only as reliable as their source. Numbers give the impression of precision, but carelessness can occur in statistical analysis. Thus, when using or refuting any statistic, take the time to investigate the reliability of the source of information as well as the method by which it was calculated.

Use charts and graphs to convey statistical information. Despite the value of statistics, their impact can be lost if they are not understood. Without clear presentation and explanation, statistics can easily overload and confuse an audience. To prevent this, use charts, graphs, and tables to organize data. Modern presentation software makes it increasingly easy to develop clear and understandable presentations that can greatly help your audience make sense of numbers.[16]

Use Commonsense Criteria to Evaluate Information

In deciding which evidence will be most effectively used in your argument, use commonsense criteria. The following questions are examples of inquiries that will help guide your evaluation.

Is the source of the information trustworthy? Whenever possible, select your evidence from sources your listener is likely to trust. Steer clear of witnesses who have given inconsistent statements, are prone to exaggeration, have a significant criminal history, use questionable body language, or seem untrustworthy for any other reason.

Is the data current? Generally, the more up-to-date the evidence, the better. Do not use an actuarial table that is outdated or an official report without the latest supplement. It is a good habit to double-check your sources just before you argue to make sure that your information has not been superseded.

Is the evidence plausible? Avoid reliance on facts that will appear to your listener to be extreme, rare, or inconsistent with normal human behavior. Beware especially of potential evidence that strikes a false note. For instance, people do not generally engage in behavior that is against their economic interest, or that puts them or their loved ones in grave physical danger. Such evidence should be relied upon only when you have nothing better and with full awareness that it may blow up in your face.[17]

Do Not Overload Your Audience

Be selective. Sometimes you are blessed with an abundance of helpful material to support your argument and will be tempted to try to use it all. Resist the temptation. Many a trial has been lost due to over-trying the case. Oliver Wendell Holmes, Jr., recommended that you simply "Strike the jugular and let the rest go."[18]

Focus on a few key points. Fred H. Bartlit, Jr., one of America's most successful lawyers, believes that you should find two or three key points and focus on evidence that supports those points.[19] He compares the mind of the judge or jury to an empty cup you are filling with coffee. The cup has a limited capacity; once you reach the brim, your material will start flowing over the side and be lost. Even when you have unlimited time to argue, winnow out weak material and select only the most salient. Approach the problem as if you were cleaning out a desk drawer: dump everything on top of the desk and put back only what really belongs.[20]

NOTES

1. Louis Nizer, *How to Prepare a Winning Case* in *The Trial Masters: A Handbook on Strategies and Tactics that Win Cases* p. 11 (1984, Prentice-Hall), edited by Bertram Warshaw.

2. Harry Caplan, translator, *Cicero: Rhetorica ad Herennium* I, ii.3 (1988, Harvard University Press), edited by G. P. Goold.

3. Lane Cooper, translator, *The Rhetoric of Aristotle* (1934, Prentice-Hall).

4. Maureen McKernan, *The Amazing Crime and Trial of Leopold and Loeb* p. 214 (1989, Notable Trials Library).

5. Herbert J. Stern, *Trying Cases to Win* Vol. 1 p. 153 (1991, Professional Education Systems Institute).

6. David S. Davis and Donald E. Vinson, *Jury Persuasion: Psychological Strategies and Trial Techniques* (2004, West).

7. William Shakespeare, *Julius Caesar*, Act 3, Scene 2.

8. *See, for example,* Weyman I. Lundquist, *The Art of Shaping the Case: Successful Advocacy In and Out of the Courtroom* (West 2004).

9. David S. Davis and Donald E. Vinson, *Jury Persuasion: Psychological Strategies and Trial Techniques* (2004, West).

10. David S. Davis and Donald E. Vinson, *Jury Persuasion: Psychological Strategies and Trial Techniques* (2004, West).

11. For excellent discussions of the admissibility of evidence, see Edward J. Imwinkelried, *Evidentiary Foundations* (7th ed.) (2008, Lexis Law Publishing); Stephen A. Saltzburg, Michael M. Martin and Daniel J. Capra, *Federal Rules of Evidence Manual* (9th ed.) (2006, Lexis Law Publishing); and Anthony J. Bocchino and David A. Sonenshein, *A Practical Guide to Federal Evidence* (8th ed.) (2008, National Institute for Trial Advocacy).

12. John Henry Wigmore, *Wigmore on Evidence* (4th ed.) (1974, Aspen Publishers, Inc.).

13. For an excellent discussion of the use of expert witnesses, see David M. Malone and Paul J. Zwier, *Effective Expert Testimony* (2nd ed. 2006, National Institute for Trial Advocacy).

14. *Daubert v. Merrill Dow Pharmaceuticals, Inc.*, 509 U.S. 579, 113 S. Ct. 2786 (1993); *Kumho Tire Company, Ltd. v. Carmichael*, 526 U.S. 137, 119 S. Ct. 1167 (1999).

15. For excellent discussions of the effective use of lay witnesses, see Paul Mark Sandler and James K. Archibald, *Model Witness Examinations* (1997, American Bar Association) and Edward D. Ohlbaum and Michael H. Graham, *Courtroom Evidence: A Teaching Commentary* Chapters 5 and 7 (1997, National Institute for Trial Advocacy).

16. For a detailed treatment on the use of statistical evidence, see David H. Kaye and David A. Freedman, *Reference Guide on Statistics*, in *Reference Manual on Scientific Evidence* (2d ed.) pp. 83–178 (2000, Federal Judicial Center).

17. For excellent discussions on making evidence work for you, see Michael E. Tigar, *Examining Witnesses* (American Bar Association) and Steven Lubet, *Modern Trial Advocacy* (3d ed.) (2004, National Institute for Trial Advocacy).

18. Oliver Wendell Holmes, Jr., *Speeches* p. 77 (1934, Little, Brown and Company).

19. *See* Emily Couric, *The Trial Lawyers: The Nation's Top Lawyers Tell How They Win* p. 5 (1990, St. Martin's Press).

20. James W. McElhaney, "The Case Against Clutter," *ABA Journal*, July 1999.

Secret 6 Appeal to Emotion

"*And now here is my secret, a very simple secret: it is only with the heart that one can see rightly; what is essential is invisible to the eye.*"

—*Antoine De Saint-Exupery,* The Little Prince

Decisions, including those made by fact-finders in the judicial process, are the product of our minds, which think, and our hearts, which feel. To be effective, you must discover and communicate your own feelings so that you can, in turn, direct the emotional response of your listener.

Emotion Persuades

Understand the power of emotion. Emotion is a powerful force in all human affairs, including arguments. When you like certain people, you are more inclined to accept what they say and to do what they want. When you dislike or distrust them, you are inclined to the contrary. Although the law seeks decisions based on reason, there is no denying that in many instances emotion will influence the outcome. Indeed, Cicero observed, "Mankind makes far more determinations through hatred, or love, or desire, or anger, or grief, or joy, or hope, or fear, or error, or some other affection of mind, than from regard to truth, or any settled maxim, or principle of right, or judicial form, or adherence to the laws."[1]

Psychologists teach that people usually make decisions by emotion and then validate them by logic.[2] Aristotle recognized the appeal to "pathos" as one of the three principal modes of persuasion (*ethos* and *logos* being the others). [*See* Secret 3, Cultivate Ethos, and Secret 4, Base Your Argument on Reasons.] Rhetoricians consistently agree that emotion plays an essential role in persuasion.

The important role of emotion may strike you as improper or even reprehensible. George Campbell, the eighteenth-century Scottish rhetorician, dismissed such concerns out of hand. "So far, therefore, is it from being an unfair method of persuasion to move the passions, that there is no persuasion without moving them."[3]

Recognize that judges are subject to emotion. Even judges, who must make logical decisions, are not automatons who merely plug facts into a legal framework. They have the same emotional range as the rest of us. It would be a "grave error," therefore, to assume they are not "subconsciously influenced by sympathy."[4]

Understand the importance of passion. The presumed dichotomy between reason and emotion is in some respects misleading. Emotion, in fact, provides motive, meaning, and context for many of the "rational" decisions people make. For example, the more intensely people care about truth and justice, the more these values will guide them to good rational decisions. Tom Peters, the well-known management expert, has observed, "Great companies, great cities, great football teams, and Nobel-winning efforts are led unfailingly by people with a consuming passion for their discipline or product."[5] Channeled properly, emotion can play a beneficial role in the decision-making process, and therefore should be strategically included in your argument.

Appeal to the heart. Regardless of your view of its propriety, an emotional appeal can be a powerful weapon in your arsenal. To achieve success with any consistency, your arguments must be addressed to the heart as well as to the mind. How, you may ask, do you appeal to the heart? What can you say that will strike the right emotional chord? You arouse emotion by contemplating the object that stirs the emotion, not by contemplating the emotion itself. You don't make someone angry by asking them to be angry. You do it by describing a situation that makes them furious. Similarly, you don't make someone sad by asking them to be sad. You do it by describing a situation that pulls at your audience's heart-strings.

Tell a Story

Include compelling detail. Framing your argument in the form of a compelling story is almost always the most effective way to engender an emotional response from your listener. Telling a story taps into your listener's conscious and subconscious and holds the listener's attention. After all, who does not like a good story? You achieve an engrossing story by using specific, sensory details that paint a vivid picture and present characters people will care about. It needs to contain a theme or plot, and should emphasize your point of view in an appropriately dramatic or sympathetic fashion. By weaving your argument into a narrative, you help your listener identify with the protagonist of your story (usually your client). This provides a favorable evaluative context while providing an overarching interpretation of the case.

Use a figurative analogy. An effective story-telling technique is the use of a figurative analogy. [*See* Secret 9, Argue with Style.] When you choose to use a figurative analogy, your job is to relate the facts of your case to the elements of the analogy. If your analogy is "the boy who cried wolf," for example, be sure that when you're finished you relate the child in the story to your opponent. Emphasize that your opponent's meritless case jeopardizes genuine cases because, due to too many false claims, people will not take a "real" case seriously. Or, read a poem such as "The Bridge Builder," in which an elderly man crosses a stream and stops to repair an old bridge. A voice suddenly asks him why he is stopping to repair the bridge when he will never pass that way again. The man responds that he is making the repair for the next person who comes that way. "So, Mr. Smith is a bridge builder also. He has brought this case not only for himself but also to help all those who will deal with the defendants in the future."

Feel the Emotion Yourself

Reflect the emotion you seek. Horace, one of the great storytellers of all time, offered this precept on his art: "If you want me to feel an emotion, you must first feel the emotion yourself." If you are cold, aloof, or detached, it will be virtually impossible to stimulate the desired emotional reaction in your listener. The story that you describe should be one that stimulates in yourself the emotional response you want from your listener. If you want the listener to feel sad, you must appear sad. If you want the listener to relate to a victim, you must create a sense of danger. This does not mean you should cry or become violent, but it does mean that you should reflect the emotions that compel such behavior.

Portray emotion with restraint. Unless you are an extremely talented actor, you will not be able to command yourself to feel a particular emotion. It must arise from within, based upon the scene or situation that your words portray. This emotion usually should not be overtly displayed, because this will be counterproductive in most legal contexts. Feel, but display with restraint. What matters is the emotion evoked in your listener.

Be Sensitive to Your Listeners' Feelings

Be alert to feelings as well as thoughts. In the famous trial of Lizzie Borden, the defense attorney, George D. Robinson, was reportedly not the equal of the prosecutor in eloquence or book learning.

Nonetheless, he succeeded in gaining an acquittal for his client at least in part because, in his final speech to the jury, "He kept in mind not only the logic of facts and of events, but the way the jury could be relied upon to feel."[6] When you argue, be alert not only to what your audience may be thinking but also to what they are feeling. As St. Augustine remarked, "I think I have accomplished something not when I hear them applauding, but when I see them weeping."

Develop emotional intelligence. You can get better at discovering what your audience may be feeling if you develop emotional intelligence. All of us, to one degree or another, continually appeal to the emotions of our listeners. Some people's emotional instincts are

Avoid Obvious Manipulation of the Jury's Feelings

In the midst of a hard-fought trial, it is tempting to use hyperbolic, provocative, or pejorative language to try to incite a jury. Sometimes, this will work; more often, it will backfire. If you have a particularly sympathetic case involving, for example, the death of a mother of small children, you may be tempted to describe intimate details about her life: how on the eve of her death, she tucked her children into bed and kissed them good night. If you go too far with details that have little to do with the issues in the case, however, the jury may react negatively to what they could perceive to be an attempt to manipulate their emotions.

more fully developed than others; a few can even read people like a book and know intuitively how to respond. Such persons may be perceived as "smooth operators" or, in the current vernacular and less pejoratively, as "possessing emotional intelligence." Those who are not so blessed must make a concerted effort to watch and listen for the emotional responses of our listeners. Some scholars now believe that people who understand and are sensitive to the emotional dimensions of life possess a capability that may be more important to success than traditional intelligence. In fact, relying upon emotions to make an important decision can be perfectly rational. How else does a jury assess the value of lost love, care, and affection in a wrongful death case or express community outrage through punitive damages when a defendant's conduct is abhorrent?

Present Emotion with Sensitivity and Subtlety

For good or ill, appeals to emotion play a role in most arguments in the legal arena, as they do in all other areas of human endeavor. To be effective, especially in the legal arena, the appeal to emotion should not be heavy-handed. It should be presented with subtlety and restraint.

Use understatement. Frequently, understatement can be the most effective means of generating the emotion you desire. If done factually and fairly, showing a "day in the life" film depicting the plaintiff's circumscribed physical abilities can influence jurors to react sympathetically. Similarly, having your client show a scar can be more effective than simply describing it. Be careful, however.

Be Especially Careful in Appellate Court

In an appellate court, use of emotion must be even more subtle. At the outset of an appellate oral argument, plaintiff's counsel introduced his client and advised the court that the client's dress was related to the injuries he suffered as a result of the explosion at issue. The court rebuked counsel in its written opinion for this "highly improper" behavior: "First, there was nothing inappropriate about Mr. Staley's appearance or his attire. Second, we would remind counsel that this court's responsibility and duty is to determine the critical legal issues before us. To the extent that counsel sought to influence the court by his comments, we admonish his behavior."[7]

Speaking too much after these sorts of presentations can undermine the impact of the presentation, so resist the temptation to reduce the impact of the demonstration by talking too much.

Use nonverbal communication. You also can use nonverbal communication to appeal to your listener's emotion. Talking quietly during a sad moment or walking toward your client while giving him an understanding smile can evoke emotion. In a stirring moment, try increasing the intensity of your voice. [*See* Secret 10, Use Delivery to Enhance Communication.]

Balance logic and emotion. In arguing, primacy should be given to the logical reasons supporting your position. Appeals to emotions are important, but they are most effective when they flow from the nature of the subject matter, not from a performance or provocative language. Dispassionate description sometimes arouses intense emotion most effectively. As Lord Chesterfield told his son, if you can "engage people's pride, love, pity, ambition (or whichever is their prevailing passion) on your side, you need not fear what their reason can do against you."[8]

Humanize Your Client

Help the decision-maker like your client. Often the most critical emotion in a case will be how your listener feels about your client. Relevant again is Clarence Darrow's belief that a lawyer's main work is "to make a jury like his client." If the jury likes your client, they will want to decide in your client's favor. Getting the jury to like your client is not always easy, but specific techniques can help.

Share personal details about the client. Usually, the better acquainted the jury is with the personality, history, and problems of the client, the more they will understand and empathize. In opening statement and direct examination of your client, let the jury get to know the client as a fellow human being. Discuss the client's family, schooling, dreams, successes, and disappointments. Encourage your client to talk about experiences with which the jurors are most likely to identify.

Coach your client about manner and appearance. Generally, the better the client looks, the more people will like him. [*See* Secret 9, Argue with Style.] Coach the client on how to dress for trial; how to appear friendly, polite, respectful and interested; and how to avoid appearing hostile or arrogant. In other words, humanize your client. Discourage your client from calling attention to him or herself. The goal is to be in the mainstream of courtroom behavior, with no emotional extremes. An occasional smile can contribute to appearing likable, but your client should smile only when it is appropriate. For example. if something humorous happens in the courtroom, your client should laugh or smile along with the jury. On the other hand, your client should not be the only one in the courtroom to react emotionally to a particular event.

NOTES

1. H. Rackham and W. W. Sutton, translators, *Cicero: De Oratore*, II, xlii (1988, Harvard University Press).
2. Lawrence J. Smith and Loretta A. Malandro, *Courtroom Communication Strategies* p. 349 (1987, Kluwer Law Book Publishing).
3. George Campbell, *Philosophy of Rhetoric*, Book I, Ch. VII (1841) (Reprint 1992, Scholars Facsimiles and Reprints).
4. Robert E. Keeton, *Trial Tactics and Methods* (2d ed.) Sec. 8.4 pp. 297, 300 (1973).
5. *See* Thomas J. Peters and Robert H. Waterman, Jr., *In Search of Excellence* (2004, Harper Collins).
6. Richard E. Rubenstein, editor, *Great Courtroom Battles* p. 24 (1973, Playboy Press, distributor).
7. *L.K.I. Holdings, Inc. v. Tyner*, 658 N.E.2d 111 (Ind. App. 1995).
8. Lord Chesterfield, letter to his son (1746), quoted in Richard Du Cann, *The Art of the Advocate* p. 149 (1964, Pelican Books).

Secret 7 Use the Best Medium for the Message

While oral advocacy—the spoken word—is the traditional means of persuasion, today the use of visual images, or demonstrative aids, is an important aspect of argument. Such aids range from a simple chart or diagram sketched on an easel to multifaceted PowerPoint presentations. Visual aids, especially visual aids with technology, can work wonders in the courtroom. The combination of high-tech imagery and low-tech witness examination often creates vivid, lasting memories in the minds of jurors. As technology has evolved, there are now more ways than ever of showing exhibits in a courtroom. It is not sophistication that counts but how well the imagery persuades.

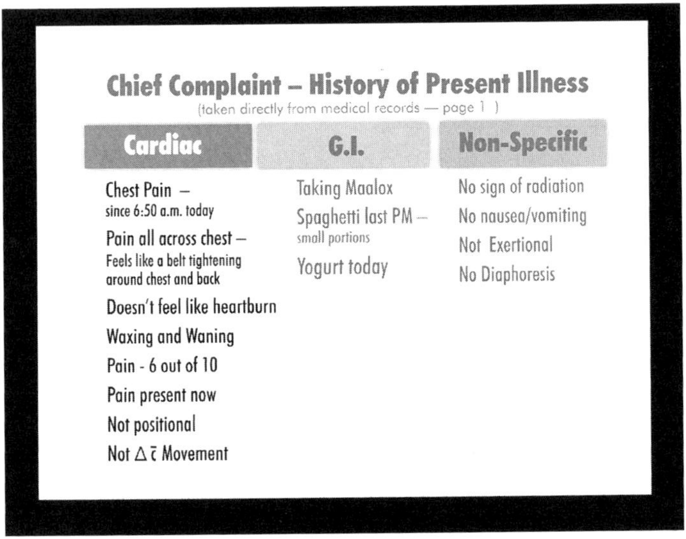

Figure 1. A PowerPoint slide.

Use a Variety of Methods to Communicate Your Message

Understand how people acquire and process information. Effective advocates understand that people acquire and process information in various ways. While now-aging baby boomers were raised to appreciate the value of the spoken word, younger jurors—and increasingly judges—are far more accustomed to visual images. Similarly, while some individuals favor logical and straightforward information, others prefer comparisons. For straightforward and logical types, charts, graphs, and technical exhibits are beneficial. Less cognitively oriented jurors, on the other hand, appreciate stories, examples, and familiar analogies. For the latter group, technical presentations of information can be counterproductive. Following text projected onto a screen or a monitor is difficult and unpleasant for those who read more slowly or prefer to review text before moving on. Any textual presentation must take these differences into account. The more you vary the ways you send your message, the greater the chance it will be received, in one version or another, by each of your listeners.

Emphasize visual aids. Courtrooms historically utilize oral presentations that decision-makers absorb aurally. Nevertheless, studies consistently show that people are far more persuaded by what they see than by what they hear, whether they are cognitive or experiential learners. Thanks to movies, videos, and computers, ours has become a visual society. With the advent of computers, people not only receive more information visually, they can control and manipulate it, tailoring it as closely to their needs as time and available data bases permit. Passive listeners are less absorbed in presentations and their retention levels are low. As Marshall McLuhan famously said, "The medium is the message."[1]

To the extent that you use demonstrative evidence to enhance the sense of jury involvement or participation, you make the learning environment more dynamic and increase the chances that your message will be received. PowerPoint presentations can help you visually recreate an event that occurred years ago and miles away from the trial courtroom.

Computer-generated visuals including animations, charts, and pictures, with important points highlighted or "called out" in the margins, can be effective aids to advocacy. Listeners are interested in this type of evidence and in many instances expect it. Use charts to depict summaries of complex information and diagrams to show the scene of the incident.

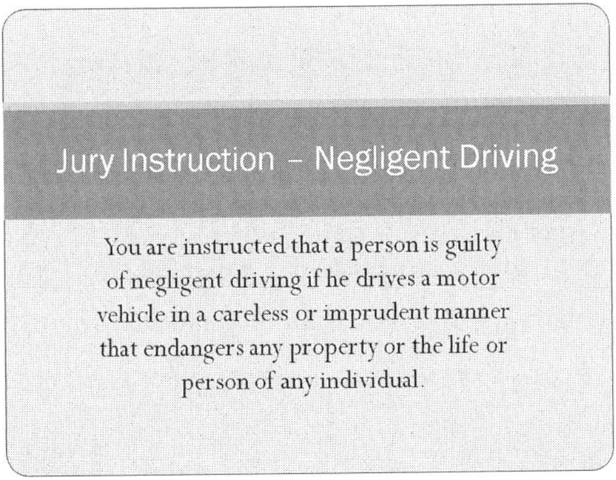

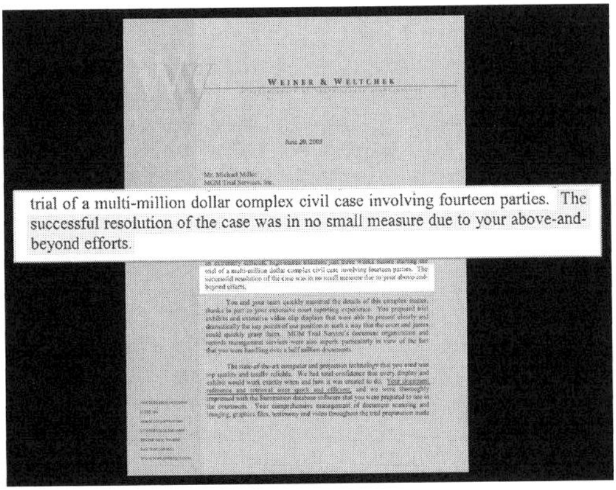

Figures 2 and 3, from top to bottom. An enlarged document, and a source document with highlighted text.

When appropriate, consider using electronic interactive white boards. If connected to an LCD projector you can digitally annotate the electronic evidence that is displayed. Interactive electronic panels can also be helpful. When connected to a laptop computer and a projector, you can edit directly from the interactive panel while facing the judge or jury. Graphs can help you explain lost profits. Graphic enlargements in color can provide impressive displays of documents. PowerPoint slides and simple or sophisticated animations can be powerful techniques of presentation. Models may help the decision-maker understand the matter in question, whether it is a building in a construction case or an anatomical representation in a personal injury case. The most effective way to work with visual aids at trial is to weave imagery into witness examinations so that the oral testimony is reinforced by the visual; the abstract becomes concrete. Everyone in the room can see what the witness is reviewing as he or she responds to questions.

Determine the appropriate demonstrative aid. As is true with the presentation of any evidence, the use of exhibits in argument should be well planned and strategic, not casual. The first point to consider is whether to use exhibits that already exist and were introduced as evidence during the trial or whether to use exhibits created solely to enhance your argument. In a contract dispute, for example, the written contract constitutes not only the formal embodiment of the agreement of the parties at the time but also concrete evidence of the parties' true intent. You can argue effectively that it is not necessary to rely solely on the plaintiff's present recollection of events surrounding the execution of the contract. Instead, the decision-maker can find in the actual contract a record of the parties' intent.

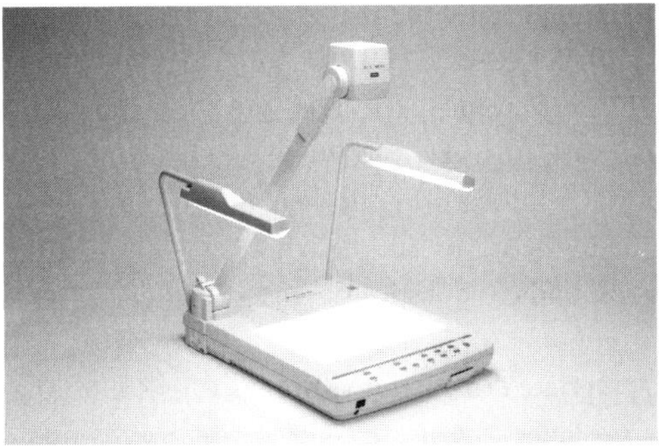

Figures 4, 5, and 6, from top to bottom. An interactive electronic panel, ELMO projector, and interactive white board.

On the other hand, you may need to create a new exhibit. Is there an object that will be difficult for the average person to imagine? A model or reproduction might hit the mark. Is the alleged sequence of events difficult to follow? A time line might help. It is important to remember that a demonstration of some kind may make vivid what thousands of words would leave blurred.

Be creative. Seek fresh and creative ideas. Consider, for example, the persuasive value in projecting onto a screen—a shared viewing area—a developing time line. Without sharing a word, the jury would participate in the development of events through a visually engaging exhibit. A "day in the life" film of your injured client has the potential to mesmerize a jury. A chart depicting the organizational structure of the businesses you represent can help the jury better understand the organization. By positioning yourself so you can use a pointer, laser or manual, on the chart and look at the jury at the same time, you can inject a new dynamic into your argument. The routine give-and-take of testimony stops and the power of visualization takes over. When you use an engaging visual aid, everyone's attention is drawn to the same place and, ideally, everyone's mind is drawn to the same conclusion.

Display Your Exhibits Effectively

Consider individual examination of exhibits. In theory, you could display exhibits to each decision-maker individually. In a document case, you can prepare individual exhibit books. It is often beneficial to circulate exhibits that jurors can touch or experience in three dimensions. Where you have but one exhibit—say, a defective oxygen mask—hand it to the jurors for individual examination (after getting the court's permission). You might even consider preparing a booklet of medical records to give to the jurors so they can follow the testimony, if you believe the evidence is important enough to merit it. At the same time you can display the pertinent page of the records on the ELMO projector or on a large poster exhibit. Keep in mind that many judges dislike exhibit displays that disrupt the flow of the trial or present logistical concerns. Handing an exhibit to the jury may raise these concerns, so you should always find out before the trial what is and is not permitted.

When displaying a document to a jury, consider all the available techniques that can help you emphasize your point. For example, you can display your document (e.g., an important letter) with yellow highlighting, or by showing two copies of the same letter side-by-side, one in its original state and the other with the highlighting.

Use Variety

However you choose to present your evidence and your argument, the challenge is to capture and hold your listener's attention. Uniformity or monotony reduces impact. Vary your use of demonstrative aids to hold your listener's attention. After an hour of videotape, move into in a colorful, high-tech PowerPoint presentation, and follow that with information on a chart that you highlight using a manual pointer. The art of balancing demonstrative aids and testimony can be comparable to directing a play or film. When you show the evidence, how you display it, and what you say about it all play a role in how effective you will be.

In some cases, the use of PowerPoint and an LCD projector might be beneficial for document display. In other cases, a blow-up of the document placed as close to the jury as the situation allows might be preferable. You might use the blow-up and have the witness step down from the witness chair—with the court's permission—and conduct your examination in front of the exhibit, thereby moving the center of action directly in front of the jury. Then, in your closing argument, you might use a projector, LCD, or ELMO to show the exhibit on a large screen.

Consider shared-viewing options. You may wish to consider the more common method of displaying the exhibit in a shared viewing area. This may be as simple as holding the exhibit in front of the jury or projecting it onto a screen.

Face the jury. When you use a demonstrative aid, do not turn away from the jury and focus your attention solely on the demonstration. Focusing on and reading a time line that demonstrates a chain of events in your closing argument could give the jury the impression that you do not know your case well and must use the time line as a "crib sheet" to recall the facts. Your credibility with the jury could be substantially impaired. Instead, use the display to supplement your oral assertions while maintaining as much eye contact with the jury as possible. [*See* Secret 10, Use Delivery to Enhance Communication.]

Assess the courtroom configuration and equipment. In recognition of the integral role of computer-generated evidence, many courts are acquiring projectors and monitors for lawyers to use in the courtroom. It is not uncommon for counsel to meet with the judge's law clerk or the court's technology adviser to discuss in advance of trial counsel's technology needs, both generally and practically. The discussion may include such matters as where the projector should be positioned and where the monitors should be located for the jury to best view the presentation. In planning how to display your demonstrative aids to their greatest effect, you must know how the courtroom will be set up.

Consider in Advance How to Respond If Opposing Counsel Seeks to Use Your Exhibits

During trial, you should be prepared for opposing counsel's request to use of some of your demonstrative aids. You may or may not find it appropriate to accede to the request; your opponent might effectively discount or reverse the power of your exhibits and use them to his or her own advantage. However, it might be difficult to say no in front of the jury without appearing ungracious. Therefore, discuss in advance how your opponent may utilize your exhibits. One of the advantages of PowerPoint, CD-ROMs, and software-enabled presentations is that they are controlled from your laptop computer. When you are finished with your argument, you can turn off your computer and return to your seat. It is possible that your opponent will have the courage to ask to use your laptop, but it is unlikely. Furthermore, it is appropriate for you politely to decline to loan delicate and expensive equipment that may contain sensitive and confidential information. Nevertheless, if the exhibit—such as an impressive illustration or blow-up of an important document—has been received in evidence, you may be unwise to object. Such an objection could cast you in a poor light as petty or unhelpful to the jury.

Be prepared for technical difficulties. If you are not absolutely confident of your ability to operate the evidence-generating computer or program, have technical assistance available. It is also very important to have backup in case there is a problem with the equipment, your program, or the courtroom facilities.

Choose among Alternative Delivery Systems

Project three-dimensional images with an ELMO projector. Projecting documents onto screens is not new. In the past, this was usually done with transparencies and an overhead projector. Today, many overhead projectors have been replaced by more sophisticated devices such as visual presenters. A popular model known as an "ELMO" is an overhead video projector, or document camera that is like an overhead transparency projector in that it projects images onto a screen. Rather than simply projecting a two-dimensional image, however, the ELMO camera can project a representation of a three-dimensional image. This can be far more effective than a simple transparency projection to demonstrate physical evidence like the failed valve or the shattered bolt.

Display documents with PowerPoint. Another popular and versatile way to display exhibits uses Microsoft PowerPoint, which presents documents as "slides." All of your documents can be uploaded into the program, and the range of possibilities with PowerPoint is limited only by the user's imagination. You can present an entire page with portions highlighted or extracted or divide presentation into multiple screens with both the whole page and an isolated portion visible in different sectors of the screen.

Create a time line with PowerPoint. If the force of your argument lies in a chain of events, you may want to use PowerPoint to create a visually effective time line. Whereas an ordinary time-line chart displays the entire sequence at once, the PowerPoint time line adds each event with the press of a laptop button, allowing the listener to participate in the development of the events.[2]

Retrieve documents with a programmable CD-ROM or DVD. You can now store thousands of documents on a single disc, with each document bar coded for immediate retrieval. The flexibility is significant because with the push of a button or tap on a space bar, you can display and incorporate into your argument any document you wish. Do you have a plaintiff physically unable to come to court? With a high-quality audio player, you can intersperse testimony from the plaintiff with text from the adverse party's deposition, point by point. The juxtaposition can be extremely engaging. The impact of these kinds of demonstrations is far superior to the most dramatic effect you could evoke with even the most passionate speech.

Replay testimony with software programs. Software programs now exist that permit you to replay testimony from depositions or from the trial itself. These programs include Trial Director, Summation, and Live Note. They can display the actual transcript as well as show a witness testifying in what is known as video-to-transcript synchronization.

In closing argument you might make the point that the credibility of a witness is poor. Now, you can demonstrate that the witness's testimony is questionable by using Trial Director or a comparable software program to show a videotape of the witness answering questions in deposition, then another tape of the same witness testifying otherwise in trial only four days previously. The impact of the visual presentation is likely to be far more potent than an oral argument pointing out the contradiction in her testimony, which the jury must recall from days ago.

Use motion visuals. Another presentation format is the motion visual, moving text or video with or without audio readily manipulated and presented by computer. Software packages such as Trial Director, Summation, and Live Note enable isolating, moving, or scrolling through text. Decision-makers can be provided with their own viewing screens, or the material can be broadcast onto a common viewing screen.

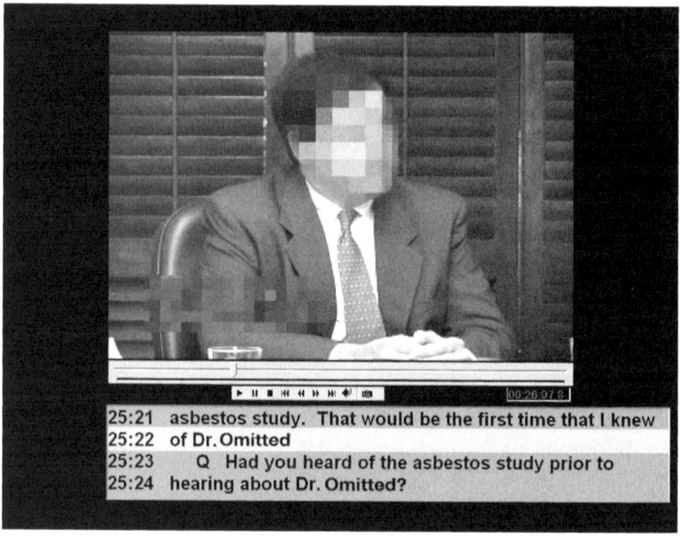

Figure 7. Video-to-transcript synchronization.

Create simple charts or graphs. Sometimes, the simplest methods of depicting or summarizing evidence can be the most effective. Charts and graphs need not be elaborate. You can help the decision-maker simplify her task by synthesizing, organizing, and summarizing the evidence and laying it out in an easily understood visual. To be effective, charts and graphs should be uncluttered, and the words, numbers, and symbols should be large enough to be easily read.

Use models. Not every case requires sophisticated technology. The simple visual aid of a document or image blown up onto a large poster board can often impress the jury. Bear in mind it is crucial that such enlargements be readable by your audience. When you or your consultant prepares such exhibits, stand back and estimate how far away the jury will be sitting from the easel or stand on which the poster board will be displayed. Design your illustration or blow-ups accordingly. Flip charts, which can sometimes be indicative of spontaneity, can also be an important aspect of communication. A witness can be asked to step down from the witness stand, with the court's permission, to draw an approximation of distance, or otherwise illuminate his or her testimony with an illustration. Sometimes the drawing that a witness makes while on the stand, or that an attorney makes during argument, can be moved into evidence.

The use of models provides another opportunity to convey your theme. Before the arrival of computers, it was common to produce life-sized or scale models for juries. You may recall seeing or hearing about a human skeleton used to illustrate a party's injury and the prognosis for recovery. Models are still considered effective demonstrative aids and have the advantage of being easily handled by the decision-maker.

Use color to organize material. Color can be used as an organizational aid to assist the decision-maker in sorting out and making sense of the evidence. If your evidence consists of items from different categories, consider color-coding the items on a chart or other demonstration device. In this way, shared characteristics can be effectively demonstrated by the same color. Bright color contrasts are effective to differentiate items or groups of items, and they're great attention-getters.

Balance the media. Whatever media you select, consider how you will integrate your demonstrative aids into your argument. A balanced approach works best. Do not, for example, show 25 minutes of uninterrupted prior deposition testimony. Intersperse your multimedia presentation with simple exhibits and your own words.

Keep It Simple

Consider the advice of experts. Demonstrative aids can be powerful weapons in your persuasive arsenal. The opportunities for creativity are numerous. Nevertheless, always bear in mind the advice of many experts: Keep it simple.[3]

With many options available for creating and using demonstrative aids, and with costs so variable, it is wise to consider discussing your ideas for visual aids with a consultant. Your consultant will review with you the various presentation equipment available; ELMO and LCD projectors, monitors, audio systems, and display screens such as interactive white boards or electronic panels. The consultant will also discuss with you various opportunities for graphics such as full-color enlargements, illustrations, 3-D animations, and the different ways of presenting documents and deposition testimony.

Weigh costs and the nature of the case and forum. Despite the advantages of state-of-the-art computer-generated displays, you may choose not to use them. Even where the costs justify their use, the nature of the case or the forum may be incompatible with such techniques. In some settings, use of computer re-creations can backfire. For example, in a small rural courtroom, a party using computer-generated evidence in contrast to the opponent's "do it yourself" charts may lose the sympathy of jurors who might favor the disadvantaged party.

Consider a negative jury reaction to expensive technology. American juries can quickly become cynical and skeptical if confronted with overly elaborate presentations. They do not want to be fooled by the use of fancy, high-priced gizmos that do not fairly represent the facts at issue.

Be wary of overly technical experts. Be wary of experts whose entire presentation is wrapped up in a high-tech package. In addition to the risk that the jury will be suspicious of expensive technology, there is a danger that the expert will become so enmeshed in the technology that his effectiveness with the jury will be reduced. Many war stories abound about the expert who, confronted with a technological snafu, lost his composure entirely and became putty in the hands of the cross-examiner.[4] The lesson is this: However much demonstrative aids benefit a case, more flash is not necessarily better. Choose your demonstrative aids with care.

NOTES

1. Marshall McLuhan, *Understanding Media: The Extensions of Man* (Reprint 1994, MIT Press).

2. Excellent sources of information on PowerPoint include Gregory P. Joseph, *Modern Visual Evidence* (2000, 2008 Supp. Law Journal Press) and Frank D. Rothschild, Edward R. Stein, and Samuel H. Solomon, *PowerPoint 2002 for Litigators* (2002, National Institute for Trial Advocacy), edited by Deanne C. Siemer.

3. *See* David S. Davis and Donald E. Vinson, *Jury Persuasion: Psychological Strategies and Trial Techniques* (2004, West); Weyman I. Lundquist, *The Art of Shaping the Case* (2004, West); Sonya Hamlin, *Now What Makes Juries Listen* (2008, West).

4. Weyman I. Lundquist, *The Art of Shaping the Case* (2004, West).

Secret 8 Strategically Arrange Your Arguments

The success of your argument will be influenced by how the listener "hears" your argument. As already discussed, the most important aspect of how your argument is heard is its substance—however, how the content is organized and how it is delivered are also extremely important. This chapter offers suggestions on how to organize the substance of your argument for maximum effectiveness.

Plan Your Argument

Understand the power of arrangement. Arrangement is to argument what generalship is to war.[1] Before engaging the enemy in battle, a general must consider how to organize and deploy his troops for best strategic advantage. Similarly, before presenting an argument, you must consider how best to organize and deploy the points you wish to make. Also, like a general, you must be prepared to adjust the planned arrangement in response to developments during the engagement. For example, if an adversary has attacked with unanticipated effect on a particular issue, immediate response on that issue may be warranted before you turn to other matters.

Choose order carefully. Research has indicated that the order of a presentation can make a material difference in the result obtained. In one simple study, a group of subjects was asked to consider a person who was described as "intelligent, industrious, impulsive, critical, stubborn, and envious." A second group of subjects was asked to consider a person who was described with the same words but in reverse order: "envious, stubborn, critical, impulsive, industrious, and intelligent." The impression formed by each of the two groups was quite different, with the first group developing a more favorable impression of the person than the second group Thus, even though the information conveyed to both groups was identical, the difference in order led to a difference in result. The lesson is clear: if you want to maximize your chance of winning, give careful attention to the arrangement of your argument.

Divide your argument into three parts. Every argument has three parts: a beginning, middle, and an end. Thought of differently, though, the three parts are an introduction, a body, and a conclusion. This three-part arrangement dates back to Plato (427–347 B.C.) and remains the starting framework for organizing an argument.

Develop a Strong Introduction

Understand the functions of the introduction. The introduction can serve several important functions in your argument, including:

1. Arousing interest so your listener will want to pay attention to your argument;
2. Developing goodwill so your listener will be favorably disposed toward you and your argument;
3. Establishing your theory of the case;
4. Establishing the theme of your argument; and
5. Previewing the subject and main points of your argument.

The functions served by an introduction will vary with the context of your argument. In a brief argument on a motion before a judge, the only function of the introduction might be to preview the subject of the motion. In that situation, the introduction might consist of a single sentence: "Your Honor, we are here on a motion to dismiss Count III of the complaint for lack of privity." In an opening statement to a jury at the start of a three-week trial, more functions will need to be served (*e.g.*, arousing interest, developing goodwill, etc.), and the introduction will need to be crafted with those in mind.

Make a strong first impression. In crafting the introduction, keep in mind what psychologists have called the "primacy effect," which refers to two related phenomena of the human mind: First, you tend to remember the information you first hear on a subject better than you remember subsequent information; second, you tend to give that first information more weight. Thus, the overall impact of what you hear first is greater than the impact of information you hear later. In the study cited earlier in which two groups of subjects heard the same descriptions of a person but in a different order, one group had a more favorable opinion than the other because the first words they heard about the person were all positive. Initial information is also important because first impressions tend to be powerful and lasting. They influence your listener's response to everything that comes after. Information consistent with the first impression is readily accepted. Contrary information is viewed with skepticism. Supreme Court Justice John Marshall Harlan observed, "The first impressions that a judge gets of a case are very tenacious."[2] Similarly, in commenting on the Karen Silkwood trial, Gerry Spence observed that, for juries, "First impressions are the most important impressions and . . . are the most lasting."[3] As the dandruff shampoo commercial reminds us, you never get a second chance to make a first impression. Make sure the beginning of your argument is as strong as possible.

Grab your listener's attention. To arouse interest and gain attention, a variety of methods are commonly used by public speakers. Consider whether one of these methods might be appropriate and effective in your particular argument.

1. **Make a startling or unexpected statement.** A statement that surprises your listener will stimulate interest.
2. **Ask a question.** By its very nature, a question directly requests a response from the listener, inducing thought

about your argument and intellectual and/or emotional participation.

3. **Use a quotation.** A relevant quotation from a famous source will usually pique the listener's interest.
4. **Tell a story.** Everybody loves a story or anecdote, but make sure it leads to a relevant point. Also, practice. Some people are born story-tellers, and others are not. Practice telling the story effectively and concisely. If you go on too long, the benefit may be lost.
5. **Use humor.** Most people also like a joke or amusing anecdote, but be sure that the situation is one in which humor is appropriate. In many legal arguments, a joke would be out of place. And if you're not a natural joke-teller, practice effective delivery or don't do it. Though it's not the end of the world, a joke with a botched punch line is no fun.
6. **Create suspense.** Curiosity is a powerful motivating factor and can be aroused by raising an issue and holding back the answer or explanation, allowing suspense to build.
7. **Direct attention to the occasion or place.** If there is any special significance to the occasion or location of the argument, mentioning that fact can stimulate attention.
8. **Appeal to your listener's self-interest.** A listener will always be motivated to pay more attention if you can convince him that he will personally benefit from your argument. Creating suspense is just one way of accomplishing this. Many people enjoy solving puzzles. If you can engage them in an intellectual challenge, they will become personally invested in your presentation.

9. **State your purpose.** A direct statement of what you hope to accomplish can set the stage for your argument.
10. **Pay a compliment.** Paying a compliment to your listener is often a good way to begin—but only if there is a sincere basis for it. Insincere flattery is almost always counterproductive.
11. **Make a personal reference.** Talking about a personal experience usually stimulates interest.
12. **Refer to the preceding speaker.** If another advocate preceded you, a reference to the prior remarks or to the speaker may make for an effective transition to your argument.
13. **Start with the heart of your argument.** It is not always necessary or advisable to have a preface or a "buildup." Instead, consider going directly to the body of your argument to address your main points first. The idea is a stark, bold start.

Grab the listener from the beginning. On the subject of how best to begin an argument, Professor James Jeans tells about a novelist who wrote for many years but could not get published. His novels began in a gentle, quiet way, developing the chronology of his tale and working up to a climax. They were good stories, but the writer remained unpublished until he decided one day to make a change. The change was not to make the plot better or the characters more lifelike but to start the story with what had previously been Chapter Three. The rest, as they say, is history. The writer's name is Louis L'Amour. Millions of copies of his western novels have been sold. Before the end of the first page of one of L'Amour's books, Jeans reports, there are "shootings, knifings, ambushes, action galore." His books grab his readers from the first paragraph. When you begin your argument, you should strive to do the same.

Ingratiate yourself with your listener. Cicero believed that a primary function of the introduction of any argument was to enable the advocate to ingratiate himself with his listeners.[4] Eliciting goodwill will predispose the audience to accept what you are about to say before you begin your main argument. This technique, known as insinuation, was used to good effect by former Senator Dale Bumpers when he addressed the full Senate on behalf of President Clinton during the impeachment trial. He began as follows:

Mr. Chief Justice, distinguished House Managers from the House of Representatives, colleagues, I have seen the look of disappointment on many faces because I know a lot of people thought they were rid of me once and for all. (LAUGHTER) And I've taken a lot of ribbing this afternoon, but I have seriously negotiated with some people, particularly on this side by an offer to walk out and not deliver this speech in exchange for a few votes. (LAUGHTER)

It is a great joy to see you, and it is especially pleasant to see an audience that represents about the size of the cumulative audience I had over a period of 24 years. (LAUGHTER) You can take some comfort, colleagues, in the fact that I'm not being paid. And when I'm finished, you will probably think the White House got their money's worth. (LAUGHTER)

I have told audiences that, for over 24 years, I went home almost every weekend and returned usually about dusk on Sunday evening. And you know the plane ride into National Airport when you can see the magnificent Washington Monument and this building from the window of the airplane? I've told the students at a small, liberal arts school at home, Hendricks, that after 24 years, literally hundreds of times, I never failed to get goose-bumps. The same thing is true about this chamber.

I can still remember, as though it were yesterday, the awe I felt when I first stepped into this magnificent chamber. So full of history. So beautiful. And last Tuesday as I returned after only a short three-week absence, I still felt that same sense of awe that I did the first time I walked into this chamber.

Note that this introduction makes no substantive argument on whether President Clinton should be convicted of the crimes for which he had been impeached. Instead, what Senator Bumpers sought, in the midst of a bitter political battle, was to elicit goodwill for himself and thereby to create a more receptive climate for the substantive argument in the body of his speech.

Introduce your theory or theme. The introduction is usually the time to establish the theory and theme of your argument—the fundamental reason why you should win—expressed as always in its simplest terms. [*See* Secret 5, Build with Evidence, Law, and Policy.] Communicating your theory and theme in the introduction of your argument gives the decision-maker a frame of reference for the myriad facts and points that will be presented later. On the other hand, there may be occasions when you may want to lay a foundation or paint other parts of the picture before mentioning your theory or theme. On such occasions, use the introduction for other purposes such as developing goodwill and establishing rapport with the decision-maker.

Preview the Substance of Your Argument

At some point in your career, you probably were advised to begin with what you are going to tell your audience, tell them, and conclude by telling them what you told them. [*See* Secret 1, Focus on Your Goal.] Putting together a jigsaw puzzle is far easier when you have a picture of the whole puzzle in your mind. Similarly, it will be easier for your audience to understand how the parts of your argument fit together if you provide an overview at the start. Your audience will be better able to follow your points as they are presented in the body of your argument, and they will be more likely to comprehend your principal message.[5]

Develop Your Evidence in the Body of Your Argument

Establish a logical order. It is in the body of your argument that you describe how your listener should decide the matter and why. To be effective, the body of your argument must be logical and coherent. Look for a pattern that logically fits the substance of your argument. An argument that is not well organized will be difficult for your listener to follow and understand, and unless it is clearly understood, your argument almost surely will fail.

Determining the proper order is sometimes one of the most difficult tasks in preparing an argument. It can even be difficult for creative writers who use a stream-of-consciousness style. There is a story told about James Joyce who, in the midst of writing *Ulysses*, was visited one day by a good friend. Joyce looked pale and was pulling out his hair. There were cigar butts all over his house, and Joyce was groaning. His friend observed, "James, you're having a bad day, aren't you?" Joyce responded, "Terrible, terrible day. *Terrible* day. Oh, my God." The friend inquired, "How many words today, James?" Joyce answered, "Seven. Seven words." The friend was surprised. "But James, that's good for you. You usually do three or four." Joyce answered, "Yes, but I don't know what order they go in!"

Evaluate alternatives. Sometimes the best order for your argument will be readily apparent from the points you want to make. More often, it will take some searching and require consideration of various alternatives. Be careful not to try to impose an organization on your argument that does not fit. Instead, look for one that flows naturally from the ideas you wish to present.

Consider chronological order. The chronological approach involves presenting your argument based on a time sequence, addressing issues in the order in which the underlying events occurred. In argument, you might invite the jury to "Come with me in your mind's eye back to the day when Linda Cooper first decided to incorporate her company." Then, discuss the several chronological steps that led to the transaction or incident in dispute. A chronological presentation has the virtue of matching the sequence in which events developed. It may, however, mask the relationship between events, blurring the impact of cause and effect. It is for this reason that we encourage you to think about the facts of your case and the points you wish to make in deciding what arrangement will most persuasively make your point.

Use an "Assertion, Presentation, and Conclusion" Approach

Within the body of your argument, you can develop one or more sub-arrangements: "assertion," "presentation," and "conclusion." For each point, begin with your assertion. After you assert your point or theme, support your assertion with a presentation, using the evidence or law. Then, refute the opposing view and conclude. Here is an example of "assertion, presentation, and conclusion."

The assertion: John Jones lacks credibility.

The presentation: Do you remember when I questioned Mr. Jones at trial? He admitted giving different answers to the questions at trial than he gave to those same questions during his deposition three months before the trial. If we were merchants and owned a clothing store, and Mr. Jones came in one year before Christmas and asked to have a little credit on the acquisition of a new sweater, we might be willing to extend him the credit. But if, in the following year, Mr. Jones comes back and asks for more credit without having repaid his first loan, we are going to have to say "no" and send him home.

The conclusion: In this case, Mr. Jones is no different than a customer who wants to have an extension of credit when he has not paid off his first loan. We should send Mr. Jones home. He should have no credit with you.

Establish a causal pattern. It is common in legal arguments to reason from a known cause to an effect or from a known effect to a cause. Such reasoning provides a useful pattern for arranging some arguments by focusing first on the cause and then addressing the effects, or by doing the reverse. For example, in a drunk driving case, the prosecutor's initial thought might be to follow a cause-to-effect order by addressing the issue of drinking before turning to the issue of driving, since the drinking would be causally related to the defendant's driving behavior. If, on the other hand, the evidence of drinking is comparatively weak, a stronger argument might be presented by focusing first on evidence of the defendant's driving behavior. The evidence might include that he was weaving on the road, that he speeded up and slowed down for no apparent reason, and that he failed to negotiate a sharp curve with which he was familiar. From these known effects, the prosecutor might then move to evidence of drinking as the most plausible cause for these known effects.[6]

Present a problem and suggest a solution. The problem-solution pattern involves presenting a problem, suggesting a solution, and indicating the advantages of the solution. This pattern is most frequently seen in arguments where the objective is the adoption of a particular policy. If you were lobbying Congress to provide prescription drug benefits to the elderly, it would be customary to talk first about the current problem elderly have with paying for prescription drugs. You would next discuss the proposed legislation as a solution to the problem. Lastly, you would address the specific advantages of this solution.

Consider Monroe's Motivated Sequence. Alan Monroe, a contemporary communications scholar, has proposed an overall pattern for argument that incorporates a refined version of the problem-solution approach. Monroe's Motivated Sequence has five steps:[7]

1. **Attention: Arouse interest and establish goodwill.** This serves essentially the same function as the introduction described above.
2. **Need: Identify what is wrong and why.** Describe the problem.
3. **Satisfaction: Propose a solution.** Discuss how a proposed policy (i.e., the solution) will work to overcome the problem and is better than other proposed solutions.
4. **Visualization: Present a vision of the future.** Consider the future, assuming first that the solution is adopted, and second that the solution is not adopted. Present a positive vision for adoption and a negative one for rejection.
5. **Action: Ask for a specific action.** The suggested action works toward implementation of the solution. This would ordinarily be done in the conclusion of your argument.

The Monroe Motivated Sequence pattern correlates well with the normal process of human thinking about how to deal with problems. It is particularly appropriate for messages seeking adoption of a new policy.

Consider a reflective thought pattern. This pattern is similar to the problem-solution pattern but differs in one critical respect—instead of being an overt advocate from the start, you assume the posture of one who is merely informing your listener and objectively helping her through a reflective thinking process. This process, as described by the philosopher John Dewey, involves five steps:[8]

1. Locate and define the problem;
2. Describe and limit the problem;
3. Suggest possible solutions;
4. Evaluate the solutions; and
5. Adopt the preferred solution.

To use a reflective thought pattern in a criminal case where the defense attempted to show the defendant had an alibi, the prosecutor might do the following:

1. **Define the problem** in terms of the conflicting evidence on alibi;
2. **Limit the problem** to consideration of alibi witnesses;
3. **Identify the possible "solutions"** as being that the witnesses are telling the truth or lying;
4. **Evaluate these solutions** by focusing on reasons to discredit the alibi witnesses and to accredit the state's witnesses; and
5. **Conclude with the preferred solution** of rejecting the defense evidence in favor of the more impressive evidence offered by the prosecution.

Compare and contrast competing claims. The comparison-contrast approach provides a framework for directly discussing competing claims. For example, in closing argument, you might compare and contrast inconsistent statements as follows: "Let's compare Mr. Smith's court testimony with what he told police when they interviewed him. Here is a chart that compares his answers to the questions asked in court with the answers he gave to the police officer who questioned him at the scene."[9] Comparison-contrast is also an inherent part of any argument based on analogy. [*See* Secret 4, Base Your Argument on Reasons.]

Use an Approach Based on Relative Familiarity

In this approach, you focus first on points that are most familiar to your listener, proceed to points with which your listener is partially familiar, then discuss points that are new to your listener. This approach allows you to start on common ground with your audience, or at least on ground that has been highly cultivated, enhancing the familiarity of the message and, in turn, the speaker's ethos. It is, therefore, ground where your point will most easily take root. If chosen well, the initial points can help you build a bridge for your listener to the new points that follow.[10]

Use simple narrative. In some circumstances, your argument can be presented most compellingly as a simple, plausible story. The term "narrative paradigm" was coined by Walter Fisher to refer to the technique of weaving an argument in the form of a story.[11] To be most effective, the narrative should develop a theme consistent with the value system of your listener and emphasize key elements of your case. If told well, the narrative can persuade the receiver to identify with your point of view and provide an overarching interpretation of the case or events. [For more on the effectiveness of telling a story, *see* Secret 6, Appeal to Emotion.]

Use a topical chain pattern when points are logically linked. In addition to the patterns described above, a virtually infinite number of topical patterns can be derived from the substance of your argument. You may find after analysis that there are three important points to make in your argument. If those points are linked in a logical fashion so that each follows from the preceding one, you have what is called a chain organization. If the links are causal or chronological, the chain organization falls into the specific chronological or causal patterns described above. If the links do not fit within these more specific patterns, then the linkage establishes a nonspecific chain pattern.

Use a parallel pattern for independent points. If your points are independent from one another, i.e., not linked in any logical way, your pattern may be described as parallel. In a parallel arrangement you might say: "There are three arguments in support of the defendant's case. First, he was not identified by any of the witnesses. Second, the evidence is insufficient beyond a reasonable doubt due to the following six reasons (give the reasons). Finally, according to the testimony of at least two witnesses, John Jones committed the crime."[12]

Parallelism, as distinguished from parallel organization, involves establishing parallel actions during the development of your argument. For example, "While Mrs. Harris is packing her clothes and preparing to drive her young son to the beach to meet her husband, John Rake is in the bar on Tenth and Main drinking and drinking, one beer after another. One hour later he is driving recklessly, weaving along the highway. When John Rake enters the tunnel, Mrs. Harris is also in the tunnel, traveling in the opposite direction. He weaves. She sings to her son. Little does she know, she sings her death song."

Limit the number of your points (the "rule of three"). Rhetoricians over the ages have cautioned advocates not to overtax their listeners and suggest that three may be the ideal number of points to make in any situation. There have even been suggestions that the number three has some sort of magical significance. The origin of this "rule of three" is shrouded in mystery. Although we are aware of no scientific research that supports the notion, there is clearly something to be said for limiting your points to a number that your audience can readily absorb. For that reason if no other, three is a good number to shoot for.

Employ frequency to emphasize key points. Social science research has confirmed that as a general rule, a statement that is repeated will be better remembered and more likely to be believed than one that is heard only once. However, when reinforcing key points through repetition, avoid restating the point in the same words, which will soon become tedious to any listener. Instead, use a variety of approaches to communicate the point, like a chart to reinforce a point that was first made verbally.

Looping is another and more sophisticated way to accomplish the same end, by weaving the repeated idea into your discussion of something new. For example, to emphasize the point that a key witness testified that the stoplight was red for the defendant, argue this way: "Mr. James Jones testified that the light was red for the defendant. Mr. Jones was sitting there in his car, waiting for the red light to turn green. He was positioned so that he directly faced the red light. In fact, he was positioned within 20 feet of the signal when he saw that the light was red." For the vast majority of listeners, you will need to find a palatable way to repeat your points if you want them to be remembered and accepted.

Use graduality to intensify your point. You can make some points outright in a general, conclusory way. Alternatively, you can gradually build up to your general conclusion one detail at a time. You could, for example, argue that "the evidence establishes that the defendant was drunk when he was driving his car. Recall the testimony of James Jones, who testified to his opinion that the defendant was drunk." Or, try this approach: "What do we know about the defendant's drinking? We know that he went to Sam's Bar at 5:30 p.m. There he remained until it closed at 2:00 a.m. He was drinking beer while he was at the bar. He got in his car and had an accident. He stumbled as he got out of his car. His eyes were bloodshot. His speech was garbled. And he smelled of booze. What conclusion can we draw from these facts? That the defendant was drunk." Note how this approach leads your listener to your key point one small step at a time. As a general rule, you can more easily and reliably get your listener to the desired destination by a series of small, gradual steps than by requiring big conclusive leaps.

Rarely Adopt Your Opponent's Order

When responding to an argument you might be tempted to adopt your opponent's arrangement of points instead of creating your own organizing scheme. Following your opponent's arrangement has two obvious advantages. First, it allows your listener to follow along easily and readily compare the respective positions on each point; second, it saves you the hard work of creating your own arrangement. These advantages are offset by one huge disadvantage: It requires yielding the design of the battlefield to your opponent. It is a rare case where your opponent's choice of arrangement will be the best choice for you as well. Instead, set your own agenda. Determine your own most effective arrangement and address your opponent's points within that framework.

Develop a Strong Conclusion

Understand the functions of the conclusion. The conclusion, like the introduction, can serve multiple functions. These functions include:

- Summarizing your argument;
- Arousing an appropriate emotion;
- Requesting the specific action you want; and
- Making a strong and favorable final impression.

In addition to the "primacy effect" discussed earlier, psychologists have identified a similar phenomenon called the "recency effect" that plays a comparable role with respect to conclusions. Research indicates that the last thing a listener hears is better remembered and has greater impact than most of what goes before, except possibly that which comes first. That is one of the reasons why having the last word in an argument is an advantage. It is also a compelling reason to take special care in developing your conclusion.

Strike an emotional chord. In 1819 Daniel Webster went before the U.S. Supreme Court to argue the case of *Dartmouth College v. Woodward*. New Hampshire had passed legislation impairing the colonial charter of Dartmouth and threatening the survival of the institution. Webster challenged this legislation as a violation of the Contract Clause of the United States Constitution. Before the Supreme Court, Webster talked for more than four hours. Most of that time, his focus was on intricate legal reasoning. At the end of his argument, Webster paused for a moment then said:

Sir, you may destroy this little institution; it is weak; it is in your hands! I know it is one of the lesser lights in the literary horizon of our country. You may put it out. But if you do so, you must carry through your work! You must extinguish, one after another, all those great lights of science which, for more than a century, have thrown their radiance over our land! It is, Sir, as I have said, a small college. And yet there are those who love it.[13]

With these memorable words, Webster concluded his argument with an emotional appeal that focused on perhaps his strongest point—that all colleges would be threatened if his position were rejected. Even in the Supreme Court, emotion is sometimes appropriately evoked in the cause of justice. Usually, this can be done with greatest effect in the conclusion of your argument, after its logical underpinnings have been fully established.

Speak to the heart of your argument. An earlier section referred to the way Senator Bumpers began his defense of President Clinton during the impeachment trial, using an introduction that helped predispose his audience to accept his message. In his conclusion, Senator Bumpers spoke directly and powerfully to the heart of his message:

Colleagues, this is easily the most important vote you will ever cast. If you have difficulty because of an intense dislike of the president—and that's understandable—rise above it. He is not the issue. He will be gone. You won't. So don't leave a precedent from which we may never recover and almost surely will regret.

If you vote to acquit, Mr. Leader, you know exactly what's going to happen. You're going to go back to your committees, you're going to get on with the legislative agenda, you're going to start dealing with Medicare and Social Security and tax cuts and all those things that the people of the country have a nonnegotiable demand that you do. If you vote to acquit, you go immediately to the people's agenda.

But if you vote to convict, you can't be sure what's going to happen. James G. Blaine was a member of the Senate when Andrew Johnson was tried in 1868. Twenty years later he recanted, saying: "I made a bad mistake." And he said "as I reflect back on it, all I can think about is having convicted Andrew Johnson would have caused much more chaos and confusion in this country than Andrew Johnson could ever conceivably have caused."

And so it is with William Jefferson Clinton. If you vote to convict, in my opinion you're going to be creating more havoc than he could ever possibly create. After all, he's only got two years left. So don't, for God's sakes, heighten people's alienation that is at an all-time high toward their government. The people have a right and they are calling on you to rise above politics, rise above partisanship. They're calling on you to do your solemn duty. And I pray you will.

End on a strong note. In the usual arguments you make as a lawyer, the stakes are not as high as those addressed by Senator Bumpers in the impeachment trial. You should, nonetheless, strive to follow his example. Do not just stop abruptly, but develop a graceful rounding-out of your case. End on a strong note that will resonate in the minds of your audience long after you have stopped speaking.

NOTES

1. *See* Edward P. J. Corbett and Robert J. Connors, *Classical Rhetoric for the Modern Student* (4th ed.) (1999, Oxford University Press), attributing the observation to Quintilian.

2. John Marshall Harlan, *Speech to Fourth Judicial Circuit*, June 24, 1955, Cornell Law Quarterly, Vol. 41 p. 6 (1955).

3. Gerry L. Spence, *On the Karen Silkwood Trial* in *The Trial Masters: A Handbook of Strategies and Tactics that Win Cases* pp. 576–577 (1996, St. Martin's Press), edited by Bertram Warshaw.

4. *See* H. Rackham and E. W. Sutton, translators, *Cicero: De Oratore* (1988, Harvard University Press).

5. For an excellent discussion of this arrangement in the context of appellate arguments, see Frederick B. Wiener, Briefing and Arguing Federal Appeals p. 114 (BNA Inc.).

6. *See* James C. McCroskey, *An Introduction to Rhetorical Communication* (9th ed.) (2005, Allyn and Bacon).

7. *See* James C. McCroskey, *An Introduction to Rhetorical Communication* (9th ed.) (2005, Allyn and Bacon).

8. *See* James C. McCroskey, *An Introduction to Rhetorical Communication* (9th ed.) (2005, Allyn and Bacon).

9. *See* James C. McCroskey, *An Introduction to Rhetorical Communication* (9th ed.) (2005, Allyn and Bacon).

10. *See* James C. McCroskey, *An Introduction to Rhetorical Communication* (9th ed.) (2005, Allyn and Bacon).

11. Walter R. Fisher, *Narration as a Human Communication Paradigm* 51:1–22 (1986, Communication Monographs).

12. *See* James C. McCroskey, *An Introduction to Rhetorical Communication* (9th ed.) (2005, Allyn and Bacon).

13. William H. Rehnquist, *Webster and the Oratorical Tradition* pp. 1, 8 (1989 Yearbook of the Supreme Court Historical Society).

Secret 9 Argue with Style

You may think of style as a way of describing an individual's personal traits, such as "animated" or "engaging." Actually, style is an important aspect of the content of your argument. Once you have decided what to say (substance) and in what order to say it (arrangement), you must still decide how to say it. Word choice, patterns of speech, and rhetorical devices are examples of style. This section explores the wide range of stylistic choices that are available to you.

Find a Style That Is Natural for You

Choose how you will convey your message. In argument, style is the form into which you put the content of your ideas, the manner in which you convey the substance of your argument. Once you have decided on the content of your argument and organized the content, you must decide what words to use to convey your argument. Your choice of words and how you deliver them are crucial elements of style. The goal of style is to convey your thoughts with precision and propriety. An appealing style may come more naturally for some than for others. Nevertheless, there are things that you can learn that will help you become innovative in developing your style. Some of the techniques discussed in this chapter will work for you; some will not. The focus here is on those aspects of style that can be learned and adopted rather than those that are instinctive. In all cases, though, bear in mind that whatever you do, whatever technique you employ, whatever device you craft, it must fit with your own personal, native style. If it does not, the effect will be patently artificial, unbelievable, and a potential disaster for your client.

Use wit judiciously. One aspect of style is wit. Jest, sarcasm, irony, and oxymorons are examples. Wit is not the same as humor. Humor involves perceiving and expressing what is amusing. Wit involves ingenuity, quickness, and cleverness in using words and ideas, and may have nothing at all to do with being funny. It involves elements of creativity and artistry. While it takes talent to be humorous, it takes imagination to be witty. Your goal in seeking to use wit in your argument is not to try to be funny; it is to try to be cleverly intriguing. Be cautious, though. As with other techniques in which the potential for misunderstanding exists (irony and rhetorical questions, to name two), be sure that your intended meaning is clear.

Use irony carefully. Irony involves the use of words to convey a meaning which is the opposite of the words' literal meaning. For example, about a vacation rental: "We didn't mind at all that the roof leaked onto the bed." To your teenaged daughter as she leaves for her first party: "Sure, stay as long as you'd like. All night if you want. That will be just fine with us." To a decision-maker: "The plaintiff's theory makes complete sense. Even though the defendant had no way of knowing what was in the plaintiff's mind, the defendant should reimburse the plaintiff for all of the opportunities the plaintiff did not pursue." Irony should be used with caution and with sensitivity to the intelligence and sophistication of the audience, lest they take the literal meaning rather than the intended (opposite) sense.

Choose an appropriate response. Like other rhetorical tools, jest, sarcasm, and irony can be effectively used, especially in response to points raised by your opponent. Engaging in a battle of wits, however, can be very risky, particularly if it is unplanned. Do not automatically assume that you must respond to wit with more wit. In the same way that you can often diffuse tension by being calm, your best response to wit might be seriousness.[1]

Suppose, for example, that your witness made a gaffe and opposing counsel understandably seized upon it—to your and your witness's chagrin. It is probably not a good idea to respond with an attempt at humor at the expense of an opposing witness. Unless you are very good and very lucky, the effort will probably fail miserably. Instead, you might remind your listener that everyone misspeaks sometimes but this does not mean the person is not sincere, accurate, and honest. By reminding your listener of her own human frailty, you can turn opposing counsel's attempt at wit to your own advantage.

Appreciate the Value of Simplicity

Speak in a clear, precise, concrete, and direct manner. In the context of argument style, simplicity means the absence of superfluous or unnecessary words. Simple does not mean inelegant—you need not use flat, uninspiring language. Daniel Webster is quoted as saying, "The power of clear statement is the great power of the bar."[2] Strive for clear, comprehensible speech that your listener can easily absorb. Effective speech is clear, precise, concrete, and direct—all things that will help ensure that your argument is understood.

Assess whether your argument is "listenable." Because arguments are meant to persuade, it is important to assess how effective they are in achieving that goal. One characteristic of effective speech is listenability. How will you know if you are achieving this goal? Ask yourself, "How educated would a person have to be in order to understand me?" Ensure that the answer to that question describes your audience. The three basic rules for crafting a listenable argument are these:

1. Use simple sentence structure.
2. Avoid long sentences, especially those with numerous dependent clauses.
3. Use polysyllabic words sparingly.

Use concrete rather than abstract words. Are your words and concepts abstract or concrete? You can describe the impossibility of two solid objects occupying the same space at the same time, or you can describe two trains, erroneously routed onto the same track, crashing into one another. You might talk about someone disclosing information gained during the course of a professional relationship, or you might talk about a lawyer tipping off his friends to dump their stock in his client's company. Concrete words are more persuasive because they help the listener develop a vivid mental image. Saying that a defendant was *negligent* is to use an abstract concept; stating that the defendant was drunk when he drove head-on into the plaintiff's car is speaking concretely.

Use verbs rather than nouns constructed from verbs. Lawyers often adopt a style that turns life's action verbs into nouns. It probably started in law school. Instead of talking about what someone decided or concluded, or what you may have decided, law students instead learn to talk about decisions and conclusions, as if they were the products of some disembodied stranger. In preparing your argument, outline for yourself what happened (in verbs), in the simplest and most accessible language possible, before you think about labels (nouns) or descriptions (adjectives) you might attach to the events.

Select Appropriate Language

Strive for propriety. Propriety involves not only the issue of tailoring *the content* of your argument to your listener but also tailoring the *type of language* you will use. No matter where your case is tried, for example, profanity and racial slurs will never be appropriate. Note that exceptions might occur only in cases where such language is necessary to the issues to be decided.

Be sensitive to the community's sensibilities. In much the same way that speech patterns vary in different parts of the country, so do community sensibilities. People in some areas might view a spouse who strayed more harshly than the unmarried other person involved in the affair, whereas others might feel the opposite. The distinction here is the difference between philanderer and home-wrecker. To be an effective advocate, you must understand the prevailing community attitudes where you are presenting your argument.

Use colloquialisms carefully. Even though society is increasingly informal, most attorneys—not to mention judges—do not use colloquialisms or slang in the courtroom. People instinctively tend to "tone up" their language when moving from a casual setting to a more formal one. On the other hand, if not overused and not crude, slang can be a vehicle for clarity when it is familiar and meaningful to your listener.[3] For instance, "sexting," a word unheard of a few years ago, can be a gentle way of describing the explicit sexual messages and photos being sent by teens.

Use clichés sparingly. When they are familiar to your listener or evoke an immediate association with the point being made, clichés can clarify. When overused, however, they can grate on the ear and memory of your listener. In addition, clichés are sometimes a crutch for a lazy mind that slips into a familiar but imperfectly fitting cliché rather than work to create an exact analogy. Your goal is

Use Inclusive Language

Speech patterns change over time. In the past, most states had workmen's compensation laws, but many now have workers' compensation laws. Policemen are now police officers, and firemen are firefighters. Your listeners will be a diverse group; the more inclusive your language, the more favorably received your arguments will be.

to choose the best words that make your points. Slang or clichés can serve this purpose but should not get in the way of your own creativity.

Use idiom for clarity. Those who travel undoubtedly realize that idiom can be an aspect of clarity in any given location. People on the West Coast speak of going to the beach; people in the Mid-Atlantic region speak of going "down the shore." Some thirsty people drink pop, others prefer soda. Some hungry people make groceries while wearing tennis shoes, others buy groceries while wearing sneakers. The best way to learn idiom is by listening to local speech.

Choose Your Words Carefully

Use vivid language. Select the words that most powerfully and effectively communicate the message you want your audience to receive. Aristotle said that you cannot create an image without thinking, and, conversely, you cannot think without creating an image.[4]

Vivid language causes people to think in mental pictures.[5] It is achieved through the use of image and feeling words.[6]

Think of the difference between saying something smells bad or reeks, or that someone was sad or devastated . . . heartbroken . . . inconsolable. The key to selecting vivid language is not to pick the most extreme word available but to select the most *apt* word. Depending on the circumstances, "sad" may be a more apt word than "devastated." A person may be sad that her regular bus driver has been transferred. But devastated? Heartbroken? Inconsolable? Unlikely. Using strong words inappropriately can constitute overstatement, causing your listener to respond, "Give me a break." On the other hand, a person whose child was killed by a drunk driver is "devastated"—a far more apt and evocative word than "sad." To create vivid images your words should have punch: the adjectives, nouns, and verbs that most effectively evoke the desired visual images.[7]

Improve your vocabulary. What is the key to effective word choice? How do you get to the point where it comes naturally and regularly? Improved vocabulary is first. In the long term, the best way to improve your vocabulary is to read a great deal, especially lucid, powerful prose by great writers.[8]

Use a thesaurus. The goal in all speech is to find the exact word to communicate your intended message. Sometimes, the search is easy because the right words are familiar. Other times, the ideas are unusual and the right words are elusive. A thesaurus can help when you have a word in mind that closely approximates your desired message but is not the exact, perfect word. But if you craft a speech and then use a thesaurus to replace every ordinary word with a polysyllabic, "highfalutin" word, your message will most certainly suffer. Use a thesaurus as an aid to, not a substitute for, your own creativity.

Avoid legalese. Many of us have spent countless hours consciously and subconsciously adopting the language of our profession, believing that if we sound like successful lawyers, we might be perceived as successful lawyers. In the process, our speech can change from ordinary, commonplace speech to a stilted form known as "legalese." Sometimes it is simply the use of certain words: "hereby," "herewith," "testator," "prosecutrix." Sometimes it is old pleading language: "party of the first part," "said individual," "duly incorporated." Sometimes it is syntax: "We would ask the court to consider. . . ." Legal jargon may impress but it does not inform.

Employ Self-Monitoring Devices

Videotape yourself as often as possible, and study the tape carefully. During the workday, replay your conversations in your mind and learn from them: was there a more vivid word you could have used? Monitor yourself to determine how you naturally speak and compare these speech patterns to those you use in court. Are they the same? If you find that your courtroom speech is stilted or very different from your normal manner of speech, practice a more natural courtroom demeanor. Studying argument is important, but actual practice is the cornerstone of success.

While the use of legal terms may be necessary at times, legalese can usually be avoided. Your goal should be to speak in terms that are understandable. Where terms and phrases must be defined, define them. A speaking style that requires constant translation will undermine your success.

Consider Classical Rhetorical Schemes to Arrange Words

In addition to the overall arrangement of an argument [*See* Secret 8, Strategically Arrange Your Arguments], the internal arrangement of word groups is also important. Classical rhetorical theory divides word groups into two categories: schemes and tropes. Being aware of these devices can help enlarge your style.

Deviate from usual word order for effect. Schemes are deviations from the usual order of words; the meanings remain unchanged. Schemes fall into three groups:

1. Unusual or inverted word order;
2. Omission; and
3. Rhythm.

Invert word order (*anastrophe*) for emphasis. If there are concepts you wish to emphasize, invert the natural or expected word order: "Respect he craved; allegiance he demanded." This has more impact than "He craved respect; he demanded allegiance." There is no "rule" about which order is preferable. Surprise can enhance the persuasive impact of speech, so unexpected or inverted word order always has the potential to provide impact if for no other reason than that it is unexpected and catches our attention. When the inversion puts the unexpected at the beginning or end of the sentence, the impact can be even greater, because under the principles of primacy and recency these are positions of greatest emphasis. If your purpose in uttering the sentence in the example is to focus your listener on behavior (the actor's or others'), "Respect he craved; allegiance he demanded" draws attention to the two verbs, "craved" and "demanded." If your purpose is to focus your listener on the qualities the actor sought for himself, "He craved respect; he demanded allegiance" would be preferable.

Use parenthesis to insert a thought. Interrupting the normal flow of words to insert a word cluster is common in writing and works well in speech. Its effectiveness comes from the unexpected nature of the addition, which may reveal the speaker's thoughts on or connections to the central topic, giving the sentence an "emotional charge it otherwise would not have."[9] "Look at the plaintiff. (It's hard, I know, because we were taught not to stare at people's disfigurements.) But look at the plaintiff and ask yourself what he thinks when he passes a mirror. . . ." The parenthetical comment not only reveals the speaker's emotion but also makes possible a thought that might be too harsh on its own. The parenthetical also acknowledges a belief that your listener might have had but not acknowledged; you can create a momentary connection and haven of comfort by making this internal contradiction safe for your listener.

Omit *readily* implied words (ellipsis). Ellipsis involves the deliberate omission of words readily implied by context: "For her, all the vacation considerations pointed to the beach; for him, to the mountains." The advantage of ellipsis is that it makes the speech pattern somewhat different from everyday speech, yet it is (or should be) easily understood. An added advantage is that, by omitting a word or words, you require the listener to supply them, which is a subtle way of keeping your listener engaged. Because of this, be sure that the missing words are easily supplied and that there is only one likely choice; ellipsis should not tax or derail your listener. If there is more than one likely version of what has been elided, do not use ellipsis!

Omit conjunctions (*asyndeton*) to create a sense of progression. Asyndeton omits conjunctions that otherwise would be included between a series of clauses: "Respect he craved; allegiance he demanded; loyalty he coveted." The conjunction most likely omitted here is "and." If the emphasis is on the final segment, however ("Respect he craved; loyalty he coveted, [*but*] allegiance he demanded"), inserting the conjunction would ensure clarity. For rhetorical flair, deliver the clauses without the conjunction but with a distinct pause—so long as there is no corresponding loss of clarity.

The principal effect of an asyndeton is a rhythmic pace in the sentence: ". . . and that government of the people, by the people, for the people, shall not perish from the earth."[10]

Asyndetons can be effectively used at any place in an argument, but according to Aristotle they are especially appropriate at the conclusion, when you may want to stir emotions with rhythm.[11] Asyndeton is sometimes hard to hear, but it can evoke a sense of progression and energy. Consider, for example, the following: "His safety, his future, his very life depended on the careful driving of the defendant."[12] A sense of movement in argument can be extremely helpful in maintaining and rewarding your listener's interest.

Use successive conjunctions (polysyndeton) for effect. A polysyndeton deliberately adds many conjunctions in close succession to communicate volume and connection. For example, contrast "Last summer I visited England, France, Portugal, Spain and Egypt" with "Last summer I visited England and France and Portugal and Spain and Egypt." Though both imply a full itinerary, the scope and time-consuming nature of the trip are more evident in the second version.

Create Rhythm

Consider the appeal of rhythm. When you are speaking with rhythm, you know it and your listener knows it—you are "on a roll," words are flowing, and the audience is captivated. Rhythm is not about speaking in rhyme or a sing-song manner with a repetitive lilt in your voice. Rhythm is a vehicle for achieving euphony—overall appeal to the ear. It is typical of emotional speech but is not limited to it. Rhythm means creating expectations that subtly invite your listener to *come along* with your speech rather than simply *receive* it.

The list that follows includes schemes that contribute to the development of rhythm. Their Greek names are provided for the linguistic purists among you, but the names are not critical to know. What is important is to realize the wide range of vehicles available to you to give your next argument some zing.

Repeat initial words (anaphora). Rhythm can be achieved by repeating the same word or group of words at the beginnings of successive clauses: "Let us go forth, let us fight, let us win" or "They planned to buy the stock. They planned to raid the company. They planned to leave the investors with nothing."

Repeat the final word or words (epistrophe). Repeating the same word or group of words at the ends of successive clauses creates rhythm: "This is going to be built by us, with us, and for us" or "Ask the plaintiff's attorney to explain to you when it happened, how it happened, and why it happened."

Repeat initial and final words (epanalepsis). Rhythm can be achieved by repeating at the end of a clause the word that began the clause: "Day followed day, week followed week, but the plaintiff saw the sky not one day and not one week."

Use the final word of a clause to start the next (anadiplosis). Repeating the last word of one clause at the beginning of the following clause creates rhythm: "Aboard my ship, excellent performance is standard. Standard performance is sub-standard. Sub-standard performance is not permitted to exist."[13]

Sequence by order of importance (climax). Arranging words, phrases, or clauses in an order of increasing importance achieves rhythm by creating a sense of climax. "The company's behavior was shameful, it was illegal, and it cost the plaintiff her life."

Repeat words in reverse grammatical order (antimetabole). "Ask not what your country can do for you; ask what you can do for your country" is a great example of the effective use of antimetabole.[14]

Use Metaphors, Analogies, and Similes (Tropes)

Enhance your presentation with figures of speech. Tropes, commonly known as figures of speech, involve a deviation from the ordinary signification of a word. Schemes involve transference of order; tropes, a transfer of meaning.[15] Incorporating tropes into your argument can increase its listenability and effectiveness.

Use metaphors to compare unlike things. A metaphor is an implied comparison between two things that are unlike in nature but have something in common. The word is derived from the Greek word meaning "to transfer." Thus, a metaphor involves a transfer of meaning, such as calling one thing by the name of something else or saying that a thing *is* something else: "On the final exam, several students went down in flames"; "The ship plowed the ocean"; "The corporate monster should be stabbed in the pocket book." Surprise and captivate your listener with the unusual and unexpected.

Use metaphors to reinforce your theme. Enhance the persuasiveness of your point by telling a story that draws parallels between the events or characters in your case and those in the metaphor. Placing your opponent's case within the story of "The Emperor's New Clothes" is a common example.[16] The following are examples of metaphors: "His hopes withered on the vine"; "The car gobbled up gas"; "The car's thirst for oil was unending."

Use figurative analogies to illustrate abstract ideas. Unlike a literal analogy, which involves a comparison between like cases or classes, a figurative analogy focuses on comparisons between unlike categories. In a trial involving the theft of trade secrets, you might weave into your argument Aesop's Fable of the little dog drowning in the well who, after being pulled up to safety by a kind person, bit the person in the hand. The rescuer then threw the dog back into the well and said, "That will teach you to bite the hand that feeds you." As you review the facts of your trade secrets case with the jury, compare them to the facts in the fable. When describing the defendant's departing in the night with the employer's customer lists, remind the jury how kind the employer was to the employee over the years, citing specific examples. Then, argue that the employee, like the dog in the story, "bit the hand that fed him."

Like metaphors, figurative analogies can help illustrate ideas, particularly abstract ideas, and are extremely effective in persuasion. Nevertheless, they do not have the same logical power as a literal analogy, where the comparison is between cases that are alike in relevant characteristics. If you are making a legal argument, argue from a precedent that is on "all fours" rather than one that is only figuratively relevant. Only literal analogies have the force of logic.

Use extended metaphors (allegories) for clarity and atmosphere. Audiences generally respond well to allegories (which are called parables when the purpose of the story is to teach a moral lesson).[17] Have you ever noticed what happens when a lawyer during closing argument says "Let me tell you a story"? There is an almost palpable sense of relaxation that comes over the jury—perhaps because the jurors know that the criticality of the information being transmitted is lower. Or, perhaps it takes our minds back to pleasurable memories of a caregiver telling a bedtime story in a setting that exuded safety and comfort. In any event, audiences like stories. The transition to an allegory need not be fancy or done with fanfare, but the effect can nonetheless be powerful.

Consider the following allegory used by the lawyer in the MCI case.[18] During the defendant's closing, the lawyer told of the old English case in which the plaintiff charged his neighbor with carelessly tying up the neighbor's goat, which entered the plaintiff's garden and ate all of the plaintiff's prize cabbages. The plaintiff demanded £100 in damages from the neighbor, who filed his defense. It was a work of art. It read, "There *were no* cabbages. If there *were* cabbages, the cabbages weren't eaten by a goat. If there *were* cabbages, and they *were* eaten by a goat, they were not eaten by my goat. If there *were* cabbages, and they *were* eaten by my goat—MY GOAT WAS INSANE." In the MCI case, the goat story became a metaphor for the plaintiff, and (so it is told) by the end of the story several jurors were laughing out loud. Certainly, not every case will provide so potent an opportunity for use of metaphor—and a humorous one at that—but remember that metaphors can be vivid, fresh, and memorable.

Avoid mixed metaphors. An example of a mixed metaphor is "He was made a sacrificial lamb for taking the lid off a can of worms." In *Dictionary of Modern Legal Usage*, Bryan Garner provides some other humorous examples: "Mr. Speaker, I smell a rat. I see him floating in the air, but mark me, sir, I will nip him in the bud." And a reference by a scientist to "a virgin field pregnant with possibilities."[19]

Do not overuse metaphors and analogies. Too many analogies or metaphors can appear staged and artificial and detract from rather than add to the persuasiveness of your argument.[20]

Use similes to make explicit comparisons. In contrast to a metaphor, which involves an implicit comparison, a simile is an explicit comparison using words introduced by "as" or "like." "The termination notice was a dagger in her heart" is an example of a metaphor. "The termination notice was *like* a dagger in her heart" is an example of a simile. Both metaphors and similes can be extraordinarily

Examine Metaphors and Analogies from Your Opponent's Viewpoint

Be sure that metaphors or other allegories fit your case. There is nothing worse than delivering a crafty metaphor that gets turned against you. When you develop a clever metaphor—and they almost always initially appear clever—examine it closely, especially from your opponent's point of view. Use it only if, after reflection, you cannot come up with a way to turn the analogy against you.

powerful in argument. Similes help create word pictures, make events vivid, and can be extremely memorable. Because similes are generally short and contained within a sentence, as opposed to being paragraphs, they can be used more frequently than allegories or other stories. The selection of the simile may well depend on what you know about your listener. If you have a musician on your jury, you might use the simile "fit as a fiddle"; but if the musician is a violin player, she might resent the violin being called a fiddle. Because similes, metaphors, and other analogies make speech vivid, they can be wonderful or deadly. It is your job to use them cautiously and wisely.

Use a Part to Represent the Whole (Synecdoche)

Another element of style involves using one part to stand for the whole. It is an oblique manner of speaking, but if the representation is carefully selected, synecdoche can add considerably to the vividness of your argument. "Give us this day our daily *bread*" and "All *hands* on deck" are two familiar examples.[21] If what you want to say is that a building was vacant, for example, naming only part of the building can create a more powerful and vivid image: "The corridors were dark and silent."

Substitute an Attribute for the Actual Item (Metonymy)

Also effective is substituting some attribute or suggestive word for what is actually meant. An unflattering example is the reference to lawyers as "professional mouthpieces." A more favorable example is "she sets a fine table" as a substitute for "she is an excellent cook who can prepare a good meal."

Combine Contradictory Terms (Oxymoron)

An oxymoron is the yoking of two terms that are ordinarily contradictory. You have probably heard those that are the butt of jokes: jumbo shrimp, military intelligence. If oxymorons are fresh and apt, they can contribute an element of wit to an argument. Because they are unexpected, they surprise; if well conceived, they tickle and thus engage our minds by their novelty. For these reasons, a well-placed oxymoron can significantly enhance your point. Used too often, they lose their appeal and thus their effectiveness.

Use a Sudden Halt in Speech (Aposiopesis) for Effect

Because it is unexpected, a speaker's suddenly stopping as if unable to continue can be an effective way to make a point. Assume, for instance, that you are describing the setting of the case: ". . . the scene of the crime . . . I cannot describe it, because it was too horrible to describe."[22] The pause increases the intensity and emotion of the moment and draws your listener into the drama.

Incorporate Only Those Elements That Fit Your Style

It is unlikely that you will use all of these elements of style in any one argument—you may never use them all. You should choose those that complement your style. As you set about the goal of improving each argument you make, incorporating some of these elements will make your speech clearer, more vivid, and ultimately more persuasive than before.

NOTES

1. Edward P. J. Corbett and Robert J. Connors, *Classical Rhetoric for the Modern Student* (4th ed.) p. 281 (1999, Oxford University Press), quoting the Greek rhetorician Gorgias.
2. Daniel Webster, Letter to R. M. Blatchford (1849) in Peter Harvey, *Reminiscences and Anecdotes of Daniel Webster* (1878).
3. Ronald J. Matlon, *Communication in the Legal Process* p. 279 (1988, Harcourt Brace College Publishers).
4. *See* Michael F. Colley, *Principles of Direct Examination* (2 Trial Diplomacy Journal, Spring 1979).
5. Ronald J. Matlon, *Communication in the Legal Process* p. 278 (1988, Harcourt Brace College Publishers).
6. John A. Call, *Handling the Jury: The Psychology of Courtroom Persuasion* p. 48, Tort and Insurance Practice Section (Spring 1987, American Bar Association).
7. Ronald J. Matlon, *Communication in the Legal Process* p. 278 (1988, Harcourt Brace College Publishers).

8. Ronald J. Waicukauski, *Learning the Craft* p. 21, Litigation Section (Spring 1998, American Bar Association).

9. Edward P. J. Corbett and Robert J. Connors, *Classical Rhetoric for the Modern Student* (4th ed.) p. 385 (1999, Oxford University Press).

10. Abraham Lincoln, *The Gettysburg Address*.

11. Edward P. J. Corbett and Robert J. Connors, *Classical Rhetoric for the Modern Student* (4th ed.) p. 388 (1999, Oxford University Press).

12. *The New Fowler's Dictionary of Modern English Usage* (1996, Oxford University Press), edited by R. W. Burchfield.

13. Edward P. J. Corbett and Robert J. Connors, *Classical Rhetoric for the Modern Student* (4th ed.) p. 387 (1999, Oxford University Press), quoting Herman Wouk, *The Caine Mutiny*.

14. Edward P. J. Corbett and Robert J. Connors, *Classical Rhetoric for the Modern Student* (4th ed.) p. 394 (1999, Oxford University Press), quoting John F. Kennedy.

15. Edward P. J. Corbett and Robert J. Connors, *Classical Rhetoric for the Modern Student* (4th ed.) p. 379 (1999, Oxford University Press).

16. George W. Ziegelmueller and Jack Kay (contributor), *Argumentation: Inquiry and Advocacy* (3d ed.) p. 241 (1996, Allyn and Bacon).

17. Edward P. J. Corbett and Robert J. Connors, *Classical Rhetoric for the Modern Student* (4th ed.) p. 397 (1999, Oxford University Press).

18. *MCI Communications Corp. v. American Telephone and Telegraph Company*, 708 F2d 1081 (7th Cir. 1982).

19. Bryan A. Garner, *A Dictionary of Modern Legal Usage* (2d ed.) p. 559 (1997, Oxford University Press).

20. James W. McElhaney, *McElhaney's Trial Notebook* (4th ed.) Chapter 20, "The Credibility of the Lawyer" p. 143 (1984, American Bar Association).

21. Edward P. J. Corbett and Robert J. Connors, *Classical Rhetoric for the Modern Student* (4th ed.) p. 397 (1999, Oxford University Press).

22. *The New Fowler's Dictionary of Modern English Usage* (3d) (1996, Oxford University Press), edited by R. W. Burchfield.

Secret 10 Use Delivery to Enhance Communication

When asked to list the three most important aspects of argument, Demosthenes responded: "Delivery, delivery and delivery."[1] Delivery—how you present your argument, and how you use your voice and gestures—can play an important role in whether or not your argument is a success. The Greek word for delivery is hypokrisis, which means acting. Today, crucial aspects of delivery include not only voice and gestures but also eye contact, body language such as facial expressions, where to stand in the courtroom, and when and how to move around in the courtroom.

Use Delivery to Instruct, Delight, and Move Your Listener

Understand the importance of delivery. No treatment of argument is complete without a discussion of delivery. According to Cicero, you achieve the ultimate in advocacy when you instruct, delight, and move the mind of your listener.[2] Your style helps you accomplish these goals, and your delivery—how you regulate your voice, gestures, and demeanor during argument—is what establishes your style. [*See* Secret 9, Argue with Style.]

Consider the response you seek. Use appropriate facial expressions, tone of voice, pacing, and gestures to evoke the listener's response. If you want your listener to feel emotion, your delivery should reflect emotion. Emphatic gestures and a strong tone of voice can help to influence anger or indignation. A soft voice can indicate a sad or touching aspect of the case. Pauses heighten attention and create tension. You might talk slowly and deliberately to emphasize the serious nature of your point, or shake your head to show disapproval. Pointing to the defendant who caused a tragedy may be effective. Consider carefully how you want your listener to respond at each point in your argument and use your delivery to elicit that response.

Use an appropriate manner of delivery. Your delivery should always be consistent with the nature of your subject and with what your listener perceives as appropriate for the occasion. An obvious example is that it would be inappropriate to inject humor into your argument when you are dealing with a tragedy.

Use Nonverbal Communication Effectively

Understand the scope of nonverbal cues. In using nonverbal communication in your argument, consider its scope, usefulness in reinforcing your verbal communication, potential to undermine communication if used inconsistently, and the importance of timing. You can communicate nonverbal cues in at least six basic ways:

1. Use facial expressions;
2. Make eye contact;
3. Move your body;
4. Vary the tone and volume of your voice;
5. Use the space in which your argument is presented;
6. Use touch.

Match nonverbal cues to your message. Few of us are aware of the many nonverbal messages we send during our interactions with other people. Even fewer of us have learned to exploit the nonverbal messages we convey. If not properly used and controlled, nonverbal cues can undercut your argument. Inconsistent cues, for example, will undermine your verbal expression and cause you to lose ground. If you are defending a criminal case and the jury observes that you sit some distance from your client or rarely look his way, the jury may conclude that you dislike your client or do not trust him. Your nonverbal cues may override your most passionate argument for acquittal.

Be courteous and professional at all times. Your behavior can be an important aspect of nonverbal communication not only during trial but also during recesses. How you act plays an important role in the projection of your image. Your listener may form an opinion about you and your case by observing how you interact with co-counsel, staff, opposing counsel, and your client. When you help your paralegal carry a heavy briefcase or smile in an understanding manner when he mistakenly hands you an incorrect exhibit,

Take Care in Interactions with Opposing Counsel

Your perceived relationship with opposing counsel is a factor that could influence your listener. If you are in a particularly serious case and during recess you are observed joking or putting your arm around the shoulders of opposing counsel, the jury could conclude that your earnestness in the courtroom is disingenuous. Treat opposing counsel courteously at all times, but avoid overly friendly behavior where you might be observed by jurors.

you communicate a message to your listener: "I am a good person, sincere and understanding." This builds upon your ethos and helps convince your listener to decide in favor of your client. [*See* Secret 3, Cultivate Ethos.]

Use Facial Expressions to Convey Thoughts and Feelings

Reinforce your point. Each of us uses nonverbal communication every day to convey thoughts and feelings. You have certainly been the receiver or the source of that look or smile that expresses a thought—positive as well as negative—without a word being spoken. A look of anger or outrage can be more devastating than the strongest vitriol or accusation. Use facial expressions effectively in argument to communicate additional thoughts and feelings about the point you are making.

Mirror the response you seek. Your facial expression should of course mirror the response you seek. Keep in mind that your facial expressions also reveal what you think about a point made by opposing side. An expression of disbelief or disappointment can be effective if not overdone; take care, however, that you do not appear discourteous or unprofessional.

Make Eye Contact

Use eye contact to signify interest. Direct eye contact is an important aspect of argument. When you look into someone's eyes, you signify interest or attention. When your listener returns your look, you have at least her full attention, if not her agreement. Combined with facial expressions, eye contact can help emphasize your point, but if you blandly gaze at your listener, the contact is ineffective. Combining eye contact with gestures and changing rates of speech can help maintain the listener's interest as well as emphasize a point.

Vary contact with each listener. It is not possible to maintain direct eye contact with multiple listeners continuously throughout your presentation, but it is important to shift and vary the contact with each listener according to the listener's response. For example, in a breach of contract case, juror number six appears to agree with you that the insurance agent consulted by your client is an expert in the field. How did you arrive at this perception? The juror nodded in agreement, slightly, when you qualified the expert. As you discuss the expert's qualifications in closing argument, move slightly toward juror number six and look him in the eye. Then make your point about how the defendant agent should have anticipated your client's needs because the agent is an expert and your client is inexperienced in such matters. As you look at the juror, match his previous gesture by nodding affirmatively and make your point. Then back slightly away and move on to the next point, making direct eye contact with another juror.

Use eye contact to establish rapport. An important aspect of direct eye contact is that your listener perceives she is being treated specially and that you respect her. The perception that you are speaking to that juror in particular takes hold, and you establish effective rapport.

Use eye contact to indicate sincerity. By demonstrating that you are prepared and need no notes and by confidently meeting your listener's gaze, you reinforce the genuineness of your position. If you argue a point with your eyes cast downward, your listener may conclude that you do not believe what you are saying.

Observe your listener. Observing your listener lets you assess his responses. If the response is not what you want, you can adjust your presentation accordingly.

Refer to your notes sparingly. Of course, if you are chained to your notes, you miss the opportunity to develop eye contact. It takes practice and skill to present your argument without being wedded to your notes, but it is worth the effort.

Use Body Language to Convey Messages

Use gestures to emphasize your point. The ways you carry yourself, move your head, and gesture convey cues about what you think and how you feel. These cues are extremely effective when you use them to enhance your argument. Do you use wide, sweeping gestures or smaller, less dramatic arm movements? The larger your gestures, the more you convey confidence or strong feelings about a particular point. An open gesture, such as holding your arms up and out, can convey open-mindedness. Arms folded across your chest can indicate a closed mind. Other examples include shaking your head over opposing counsel's claim to have met the burden of proof; strong arm gestures while emphasizing a point; removing your eyeglasses to indicate gravity; or dismissively waving your hand as if sweeping away crumbs when referring to the plaintiff's unfounded claim.

There are an infinite number of ways to use these physical cues. When you refer to the defendant, point in her direction and comment, "All because of the negligence of that large company whose president told us they were the best in the business." As you elaborate on the damages suffered by your client, continue to repeat the comment. In the nineteenth century, Sir Edward Marshall Hall, Q.C., later Lord Chancellor of England, was reportedly the first advocate to hold out his hands to imitate the scales of justice. He then demonstrated that the prosecution had not met the burden by raising and lowering his arms.

Consider your own natural proclivities. Using gestures and movements of your body to anchor significant points can be very effective so long as these gestures do not appear contrived. One way to improve your use of cues in argument is to consider how you use them in your regular conduct. Once you have identified how you naturally use cues, transfer them to the courtroom. It may be helpful to practice before a mirror to fine-tune them.

Appear confident at all times. You must be in control of your nonverbal cues to avoid sending your listener an unintended message. While opposing counsel emphasizes a point during her argument, you may start fidgeting and look worried. The listener who observes this conduct may conclude that you recognize defeat or have little confidence in your case. Because your listener will observe you even when you are not presenting, take care to appear confident at all times. Suppose that, to your surprise, the judge sustains opposing counsel's objection during your closing argument. The jury will listen to your response and also note your body language. Are you scowling, frowning, or expressing anger or uncertainty? Or, are you smiling and moving seamlessly and confidently forward without skipping a beat?

Use good posture. Your posture is important and can communicate your feelings about your case. When seated, sit up straight. Do not slouch or lean back. When arguing, stand erect. Using good posture demonstrates your confidence in the rightness and fairness of your legal position in the case.

Use Your Voice for Impact

Modulate your voice. During your argument, raise or lower the pitch, volume, and intensity of your voice. Of course, voice modulation must be appropriately related to content—do not shout in anger when whispering would better demonstrate remorse. One effective technique is to use the same volume and intensity of voice whenever you refer to particular facts or individuals during your argument. You can swing from one volume to another to emphasize particular points.

You can also use your voice to play off of opposing counsel's argument. In closing argument in a case involving false arrest, defense counsel stood back from the jury and spoke in a loud, booming voice. Plaintiff's counsel, in rebuttal, moved close to the jury and spoke very softly, explaining that the truth need not be shouted. Make sure you use vocal cues in a manner that comes across as natural and uncontrived. When you combine voice modulation, eye contact, and appropriate body movements, you enhance the power of your argument and hold the attention of your listener.

Pace your speech. Changing your rate of speech to match the mood of the moment can be very effective. Slow down and speak deliberately when emphasizing a serious point. When asking a rhetorical question, pause for effect before moving on. In the trial of Bruno Richard Hauptman for kidnapping the Lindbergh child, defense counsel asked a series of rhetorical questions, pausing after each to give the jury the chance to think about the answer. Pressing the theory that the defendant was a scapegoat, he asked, "If the defendant, as they charge, tore the thumb guard from the sleeping garment, why didn't he tear off both? Where is the other one?" After pausing to allow the jury to think, defense counsel argued the illogic of this evidence.[3]

Use good diction and pronunciation. Sophisticated use of voice includes diction and pronunciation. Your choice of words and the way you pronounce them profoundly affect your listener. When you speak clearly and at a comfortable pace, without "ums" and "ahs," you enhance the quality of your presentation. Clarity of speech promotes understanding and holds your listener's attention.

Use Touch to Show Sincerity

Show sympathy for your client. Touching, such as shaking hands with your client or placing a comforting arm on his shoulder, can convey your support and genuine belief in his cause. If the jury likes you and observes that you like your client, you can reinforce your client's credibility.

Enhance your ethos. A sympathetic touch on the shoulder of your co-counsel or paralegal can demonstrate your own humanity, which will lend credibility to your argument.

Use Space Appropriately

Know the judge's rules. How you use space is an important aspect of delivery. Where to stand and how freely you can move in the courtroom are governed in part by court rules and the predilections of individual judges. If you have questions, it is wise to consult the rules and the judge's staff before you present your argument. In one jurisdiction, the judge does not allow counsel to stand when the jury enters and departs and reprimands counsel if they do so—in the presence of the jury. Knowing the judge's preference can avoid this type of embarrassment. (Of course, standing as the jury enters and departs is a good nonverbal mode of communication—it shows respect). The milieu of the appellate court requires a more formal approach than mediation or jury argument. When arguing from a lectern, stay behind the lectern instead of moving around. Be aware of the rules governing location and occasion.

Stay seated for an informal approach. Consider the effect of remaining seated when the situation allows. For example, conducting voir dire from a seated position may convey less formality and create a more relaxed atmosphere.

Consider Where to Stand

Where you stand at various points in the trial is also an aspect of delivery. Compare, for example, standing behind a lectern and reading an argument with standing before the jury box and arguing without notes. The former can be flat and one dimensional, whereas the latter is exciting and enlivening. When you are required by the court to stand behind a lectern, you may be permitted to step to the side so long as you do not stray far from the lectern. Movement is helpful when emphasizing a point or changing topics, but it is still important to use eye contact and appropriate gestures, especially from a lectern. Body positions can demonstrate control and competency and heighten persuasiveness. Moving from one juror to the next in closing argument, making direct eye contact, gives a powerful impression that you care about each juror and that you are speaking from the heart rather than a script prepared for the case. Of course, you may need to review notes from time to time; glance at them and continue with your presentation without a long, disruptive pause.

Keep an appropriate distance. The use of space involves considerations of boundaries and how society uses space in interactions. You probably stand or sit further away from someone when conducting business than when being social. Approaching the jury rail when the court allows you to do so may invade the personal space of the jurors or may effectively create a bond. You can often pick up clues from the jurors—a look of discomfort when you approach the rail, for example. There are no uniform rules to how close is too close, but consider allowing several feet, depending on the size of the courtroom and the relative distance between counsel and the jury.

Use Timing Effectively

Do not overuse gestures. Often the effectiveness of nonverbal cues depends on timing. Removing your glasses and shaking your head with a despondent look while commenting on a particular incident can reinforce your point. Do not do so repeatedly, however, or its effect may be lost.

Take cues from your listener. It is important to stay alert for nonverbal signals or cues from your listener. [*See* Secret 2, Tailor Your Argument to the Decision-Maker.] Interpreting your listener's response is an important element of timing that can help you know *when* to adjust your argument to help a listener who appears to have trouble following it, or to shift emphasis to a matter that will be better received.

Consider the Effect of Your Appearance

Make a good first impression. Although it may appear self-evident, you should appreciate that appearance is an important means of nonverbal communication. During the first moments of an argument or opening statement, judges, juries, and arbitrators observing you for the first time will form impressions of you and your case. Your appearance and demeanor may influence those first impressions. If you seem offensive at the outset, your image may be tarnished throughout your argument, lowering your ethos and your persuasiveness.

Consider regional differences. Standards of dress vary. Styles of dress in the western part of the country are often more relaxed than those in certain sections of the East Coast. While there is no standard dress code to recommend, you must consider your dress and appearance before every argument, taking into account the customs and general standards of the area. This includes the way your audience expects lawyers to look. Many lawyers avoid bow ties based on the belief that juries will not trust someone wearing a bow tie, but those who argue appellate cases or nonjury trials have no hesitation to wear them. Although you might prefer more casual and colorful attire at times, traditional suits usually represent competence and professionalism. Be conservative in a way that is comfortable for you, consistent with your own personal style, and compatible with your audience's expectations.

Acceptable language may also vary from one jurisdiction to the next. For example, a jury in Los Angles may not be familiar with the term "waterman," while juries in Maryland would know that a waterman is someone who fishes or crabs on the Chesapeake Bay. Referring to the jurors as "folks" might suggest disrespect or lack of formality in one jurisdiction, but be perfectly acceptable in another. When trying a case in an unfamiliar location, familiarize yourself with the community and its customs so you will not be perceived as an out-of-towner.

Choose jewelry carefully. Sparkling jewelry can be distracting and inappropriate in the courtroom. Some trial lawyers will not wear jewelry of any kind, including cuff links, when arguing before a jury on the theory that expensive-looking jewelry creates a gulf that interferes with having the jury "identify" with the lawyer.

Appear well organized. The way you arrange your material on the table or lectern is a significant factor in your appearance. A neatly arranged table conveys preparedness, organization, and control. If you are always groping for the opinion on point or a particular exhibit, you can lose credibility.

Be yourself. There may be room to disagree about specifically what to wear and how to look; however, there is no disagreement that appearing natural and comfortable helps engender confidence.

Use Subtlety and Restraint

Avoid excessive gesturing. Use restraint in your delivery. How often have you attended a lecture or speech where the speaker talked with his hands? Avoid this mistake in your argument. Gesture when appropriate, but avoid excessive and overly dramatic gestures, which can distract and annoy. Use moderation in all aspects of delivery.

Avoid Poor Delivery Traits. Failing to follow all of our suggestions for excellent delivery will not necessarily result in a poor delivery; only you know what works for you, and your delivery will likely change on a case-to-case basis. There are some tendencies, however, that you should always avoid, however you deliver your message. Repeating the answer each time a witness answers a question, or saying "ok" after each answer, are examples of poor delivery traits. Additional examples include reading your notes continuously; looking down at the floor the entire time you present your closing argument; removing and replacing your eyeglasses; or pointing a pencil at the listener. You can improve your delivery through practice, and should also consider video recording yourself. Watch yourself deliver an argument and you can adjust to avoid mistakes in the courtroom.

NOTES

1. *See* Edward P. J. Corbett and Robert J. Connors, *Classical Rhetoric for the Modern Student* (4th ed.) p. 22 (1999, Oxford University Press).

2. *See* H. Rackham and E. W. Sutton, translators, *Cicero: De Oratore* (1988, Harvard University Press).

3. Sidney B. Whipple, editor, *Trial of Bruno Richard Hauptman* p. 537 (1989, Notable Trials Library).

Secret 11 Engage Your Listener

Holding the attention of the jury or judge can be challenging in any case, particularly if the case involves technical or complex facts and issues. Without gaining your audience's attention, it is difficult to persuade them. Here are some techniques you should consider.

Lead Your Listener to the Desired Conclusion

Engage your listener in the thought process. Anyone who has ever raised children knows that you prefer they adopt your rule rather than simply follow it because they will be more likely to adhere to it when you are not watching. Ordering a child to follow a rule is easy; you simply announce your preference and offer a stick or a carrot to secure compliance. Getting a child to adopt your rule is more difficult. Sometimes, the child will adopt a rule simply because you announce it; more often, this requires interaction; it requires teaching; it requires engaging the child in the thought process. The same is true for the adults to whom you argue. The challenge of making an effective argument is convincing your listener that the position you advocate should become his embraced position. To the extent that you can engage your listener in the thought process, you enhance the chances that he will embrace your conclusion. He will hold these convictions more solidly and will be better prepared to resist counterattacks by your opponent.

Avoid demands or pleas. You could demand that your listener draw a specific conclusion: "You must do thus and so" or "Only an irrational person would find otherwise." Because people dislike being ordered to do something, phrases such as these tend to alienate them and can often create a boomerang effect.[1] Some lawyers beg or plead—explicitly or implicitly—seeking to evoke sympathy: "Please, examine your consciences." "How will you feel if you don't rule in such a way?" Demands and pleas can create distance between you and your listener—between your desired conclusion and your listener's state of mind. Rather than demanding or pleading for a particular result, it is much more effective to lead or guide your listener to the desired conclusion.

How do you lead your listener? Consider the concepts of pacing, understatement, rhetorical questions, and embedded commands.

Pace Your Argument

Pace to your listener's mood and mindset. In oral argument, pacing determines the listener's state of mind and acknowledges that position. It leads your listener to agreement with your point of view. If you can determine how your listener is reacting to your argument, you can increase rapport by acknowledging your understanding of your listener's feelings or ideas and either reinforcing that position or leading your listener to a different position.

For example, when one spouse is tired and would prefer to skip a business obligation, the other spouse might say, "I know you're tired and would prefer not to go, but it would mean a lot to me professionally if we make even a brief appearance." In a mediation, plaintiff's counsel might begin by saying, "I know the defendant is angry about the publicity this case has generated. This reaction is understandable; the coverage has been brutal. Nevertheless, the public is angry that the defendant would ignore safety for the sake of profits. Of course, the press does not know all the facts, so what we should do is work toward an outcome that compensates the plaintiff while allowing the defendant an opportunity to reclaim its reputation."

In both of these examples, the speaker with the agenda to persuade "paced" his listener and his argument by acknowledging his listener's mindset, validating it, and using that validation as a point of departure. By using this technique, you can encourage agreement with your view rather than demand it.

Pace to create a receptive environment. When you pace and develop a rapport with your listener, you create a receptive environment for persuasion. Centuries ago, the great Roman teacher of rhetoric Quintilian advised his students to gauge the temper of the judge. When the judge or jury appears impatient and eager to move to another point, you should consider doing so. If not, explain that you may be spending what seems like an inordinate amount of time on a particular point but you are doing so for good reason. Then explain your reasons, which may include for example preservation of the record or the establishment of a crucial point.

Pacing enables you to engage your listener's mind and demonstrate that you perceive how he is reacting. Telegraph that you understand your listener's mindset but want him to meet you halfway to explore why your point is worthy of consideration. Of course, to be an effective pacer you must correctly interpret your listener's mindset. This is one of the greatest challenges for you as an advocate. Experience, intuition, common sense, study, and reliance upon consultants when appropriate contribute to your ability to interpret correctly how your listener is processing information and reacting to you and your argument.

Allow Your Listener to Participate in the Solution

Most people find a measure of satisfaction in being edified. Figuring out for yourself the answer to a problem, the solution to a dilemma, or the way something operates provides a measure of satisfaction that is greater than having someone tell you the answer. Because your listener must embrace your position with sufficient conviction to defend it against attack by your opponent, it is important that the decision be solidly formed. When a listener only tentatively arrives at a conclusion, he is likely to be moved from it with minimal effort on the part of a detractor. The challenge in preparing an argument is to identify the best manner to allow, not force, your listener to conclude that your position is right.

Use understatement. Understatement permits your listener to believe that she is solving the problem or resolving the case by resorting to her own thoughts and ideas. For that reason, understatement can evoke stronger feelings of involvement or commitment than the listener might have if she were exhorted to adopt a particular position.

Use the power of suggestion. Suggestion is similar to understatement in that it allows your listener to have the sense of being involved in solving the problem. It can induce a sense of teamwork.[2]

Use the technique of suggesting an idea (praeterition). Classical advocates like Cicero used the technique of praeterition as a way to engage listeners. The device permits the user to suggest an idea while pretending not to do so. For example, in closing argument, you might state: "I will not mention the flimsy alibi defense that Jones offered." Another example is "I shall pass over commenting on the defendant's flight from the scene; after all, defendant testified that he is innocent. I shall also pass over defendant's testimony that he did not see the victim the previous evening despite the avalanche of testimony to the contrary."

Ask Rhetorical Questions

A rhetorical question is one asked not to elicit an answer but to make a point.

Use rhetorical questions to lead your listener. Posing rhetorical questions is an excellent way to lead the listener. They can cause your listener to pay closer attention and permit him to think, learn, and form conclusions that he can embrace as his own, both intellectually and emotionally.[3]

Evaluate each rhetorical question carefully. Like other elements of style, the use of rhetorical questions has rules. Be sure that you know how your listener will respond to the question.[4] Do not pose questions that have potential answers that do not favor your side. Rhetorical questions can also highlight weaknesses in your case, so be sure that they raise only issues you intend to address. Remember to examine each rhetorical question from your opponent's perspective. Does your opponent have an effective response, either obvious or subtle? Evaluate each rhetorical question to make sure it works to your benefit.

Pose "*yes*" or "*no*" questions. Rhetorical questions work best when they pose "yes" or "no" questions and the anticipated answer is obvious and inexorable. "Does it make sense that a person with an urgent need to be in New York City would leave Washington, D.C., and drive south to Atlanta?" "If the plaintiff knew that the window flower box was unsafe, would he have sat still while his six-year-old child swung back and forth from it?" "Don't we know that when the defendant sent $500,000 to the Internal Revenue Service it was because he felt the winds of the investigation blowing against the back of his head?" The advantage of a question answerable by "yes" or "no" is that it allows the listener to decide and quickly resume listening. A question like "What do you think might have accounted for the defendant's decision to go forward with production?" invites the listener to consider the potentially numerous possibilities and, even worse, to evaluate each. All this takes time and mental effort—which means the listener is not paying attention to the next sentence, paragraph, or section of your argument.

Use Thought-Provoking Questions with Care

The thought-provoking rhetorical question must be used carefully in legal argument. Do not ask a question that can easily be answered in a way that hurts your case. Do not ask a question that must be answered in a way that helps you but that requires substantial reflection in order to come to the right answer. Also, do not forget that there are rules against inciting undue sympathy on the part of jurors and against too patently putting the jurors in the position of the parties to the case, so the questions should not pander to these goals. With these limits in mind, however, using a provocative rhetorical question that invites serious thought and reflection can be an exciting way to begin an argument.

Ask challenging questions. Some believe there is a time for asking challenging rhetorical questions that do not demand an immediate answer. That time may be early in your argument, perhaps at the very beginning. Such a question violates the "yes" or "no" rule but compensates by being an extraordinary attention-getter. Think how effective it might be to begin a speech with a provocatively phrased, theme-screaming rhetorical question. "Have you ever thought about what it might be like to be wrongly accused of raping someone?" Both the tactic and the immediate focus create an element of surprise that engages the listener.[5] This tactic also employs the theory of primacy; the theme is made all the more prominent by its early placement.

Use Embedded Commands to Communicate

Use embedded commands to suggest. Embedded commands engage both the conscious and unconscious minds. The embedded command identifies the specific communication and transmits it to the unconscious mind in a way that is acceptable to the conscious mind. People do not like to be told what to do. Embedded commands are like sugar coating on medicine. Like the rhetorical question, the embedded command tells the listener how to think, in an indirect and subtle way.

Preface a command with a tentative phrase. The technique of embedded commands involves prefacing the command with a tentative or permissive phrase. In a case involving a breach of contract and alleged wrongful termination, you want the jurors to conclude that the defendant had just cause to terminate the plaintiff because the plaintiff was an ineffective manager. You might say, "I wonder how many people would employ someone in a management capacity who would arrive one hour late every single day?" The permissive preface "I wonder" is an embedded command. Essentially, you are telling the jury that your client was right to discharge the plaintiff: the plaintiff was always late for work. Rather than simply stating that fact, the embedded command includes a permissive statement that is compatible with a listener's experiences and range of ideas. The embedded command can be used effectively with the technique of understatement, as in the previous example.[6]

Use Anchors to Involve Your Listener

Anchoring emphasizes a particular point or theme in your argument without your restating it. It elicits a desired emotional response from your listener without directly asking for it. For example, at a point of heightened intensity in your argument involving a motor vehicle collision, you can lower your voice, speak slowly, stand in a particular spot, and look at the jury. Whenever you want to elicit the mood created by your prior description of the collision, speak, stand, and look at the jury in the same manner. When you anchor, your listener is conditioned like Pavlov's dog to respond in the desired fashion. You can anchor points by using your voice or gestures while taking listeners through your description; later in your argument, you can use the anchor in place of the full description to emphasize the point you wish to make.[7]

Remember that a well-crafted argument has persuasive content and employs persuasive language. Just as important, it is proffered in a persuasive manner; not in a commanding fashion, but in an alluring or suggestive fashion. The well-crafted argument engages the jury and judge by appealing to various types of listeners: those who learn visually; those who learn by hearing; those who learn by analyzing; and those who react primarily to emotion. Therefore, you should use the various techniques of argument to engage all of the various types of listeners. For example, a rhetorical question may be helpful in persuading an analytical listener. On the other hand, use of anchors may appeal more to a listener who responds best on an emotional level.

NOTES

1. David S. Davis and Donald E. Vinson, *Jury Persuasion: Psychological Strategies and Trial Techniques* (2004, West).

2. *See* James C. McCroskey, *An Introduction to Rhetorical Communication* (9th ed.) (2005, Allyn and Bacon).

3. Donald E. Vinson, *Jury Trials: The Psychology of Persuasion* p. 113 (1986, Michie).

4. Ronald J. Matlon, *Communication in the Legal Process* p. 278 (1988, Harcourt Brace College Publishers).

5. Edward P. J. Corbett and Robert J. Connors, *Classical Rhetoric for the Modern Student* (4th ed.) pp. 268–269 (1999, Oxford University Press).

6. *See* Lawrence J. Smith and Loretta A. Malandro, *Courtroom Communication Strategies* pp. 366–373 (1987, Kluwer Law Book Publishing).

7. *See* Lawrence J. Smith and Loretta A. Malandro, *Courtroom Communication Strategies* pp. 405–406 (1987, Kluwer Law Book Publishing).

Secret 12 Immunize and Refute Opposing Points

Immunization and direct refutation are two important aspects of persuasion that, while understood by many, are mastered by few. You must understand the opposing case and know how to take the wind out of your opponent's sails. What follows are some techniques that will help you appreciate and utilize this secret.

Use Refutation to Undermine Your Opponent's Case.

Understand your opponent's case. When Abraham Lincoln was asked his secret for winning lawsuits, he replied that he understood the opposition case better than the opposition understood its own case.[1] Knowing the opposition's case involves understanding both its strengths and its weaknesses. In refutation, you reveal weaknesses in your opponent's argument in a way that makes it unacceptable to the decision-maker. Methods of refuting your opponent's argument can include immunization, direct response, and rebuttal. The substance of refutation is based on the logical and evidentiary concepts discussed in earlier chapters. [*See* Secret 4, Base Your Argument on Reasons and Secret 5, Build on Law, Evidence, and Policy.]

Consider all possible points to undermine your opponent's case. Bear in mind that an argument may be weak in a variety of ways. This chapter identifies many of the most common types of weaknesses, but the discussion is suggestive rather than exhaustive. As you plan how to refute your opponent's argument, continue to watch for other points that weaken your opponent's case and strengthen your own case.

Be selective as to which points to refute. Selectivity requires a complete grasp of the case and an understanding of what will most impress your listener. Time constraints may play a role in choosing which of your opponent's points to refute. Another factor is the attention span of your listener, particularly if you are presenting argument in rebuttal. By the time you present your rebuttal, your listener may well be saturated.

Use "Blocking" to Identify Points to Refute

Blocking involves writing the opponent's main points in an outline or diagram form, followed by a list of refutation points. Once you have blocked your opponent's argument, you can easily select the points you need to refute and the specific method of refutation that will work best. Although it is best to undertake the exercise of blocking prior to the actual argument, a variation of the technique can be used during argument. Simply reserve the left or right margin of your note-taking page for points of refutation. When you hear a point you wish to refute, write it down and draw a block around it. When you review your notes to prepare for response or rebuttal, your blocked notes will significantly assist you.

Immunize Your Own Argument

Explain weak points. When you are the first to present an argument, it is important to provide an explanation of any weak points in your case before your opponent has a chance to address them. This approach strengthens your argument because you can persuade your listener that you have considered all sides of the case and are convinced that your position is the correct one. It can have the added benefit of putting your opponent off balance so that he cannot present an effective response to your argument.

Forewarn Your Listener about What Your Opponent Will Argue

There are two basic types of immunization: forewarning and inoculation. Forewarning involves alerting your listener to what you anticipate your adversary will argue. In a personal injury case where contributory negligence is a defense, you might argue: "The defense will contend that Mr. Smith was also negligent and that his contributory negligence bars his right to recover from the defendants." Alerting your listener to the opposing point of view prepares your listener to absorb the opponent's attack without abandoning your point of view. Inoculation involves forewarning followed by some explanation of why the adversary's argument is defective.

The full "dose" of explanation can be reserved for a subsequent time, i.e., rebuttal, although it is sometimes better to give a full explanation at the outset of your argument. This would be particularly true when you know the defense is going to raise a crucial issue in the case, and you want your listener to hear your version and explanation first. In the Florida presidential election trial argued December 2000, David Boies, arguing on behalf of Al Gore, forewarned Judge Saul that Barry Richard, speaking on behalf of George W. Bush, would argue that the Florida statute did not permit the court to order certain votes to be counted. Boies then explained why Richard was wrong. Boies made the most of his opportunity to explain away his adversary's point before it was raised and in that way set the stage for the court to consider Richard's argument "in the proper context."

Use direct and indirect immunization methods. Consider this example of immunization. The plaintiff states, "The defendants will argue that they did not breach the contract, but that Mr. Smith, the plaintiff, failed to fulfill his own contractual obligations. Thus, the Jones Company had no choice but to select another supplier. We will demonstrate that Smith did fulfill his obligations." Other times, your immunization can be more subtle but just as effective: "In this case we will demonstrate that Jones breached the contract, and that Smith performed each and every requirement under the contract. Some of the requirements, known as conditions precedent, obligated us to have a performance bond, additional insurance in place, and financial information available for inspection. All this Smith did." In the latter example, counsel did not suggest to the listener that opposing counsel would argue that conditions precedent were not satisfied. Instead, counsel subsumed the counter argument into the main argument and seamlessly included the opposing point or refutation without identifying it as an opposing point. Later, when opposing counsel argued that the conditions precedent were not satisfied, the listeners were prepared to doubt that statement because they had previously heard plaintiff's counsel state otherwise.

Be selective as to points to immunize. Not every point should be immunized; use your best judgment in the selection of which points require it. If you overdo immunizing, your argument will lose its force and appear disjointed. Your listener may even conclude that you do not have a case because you appear to be overly worried about your adversary's argument. Striking the proper balance is essential to deflect the opposition and maintain a vigorous theme to advance your cause.

Support Your Direct Response by Building a Strong Case

Understand that refutation is only part of the case. The underpinning of direct response must be the strength and appeal of your own case. Before you attack your opponent's argument, you must first have built your own superior case—a case that stands on its own legs. There is a story that many years ago when Robert Jackson was Solicitor General of the United States, he overheard a young lawyer in the hallway inquire anxiously whether the appellant's brief had been received. The young lawyer expressed eagerness to begin the government's brief. Jackson called out, "What? Doesn't the government have a case in this one?" Jackson was making the point that the defense must have a theme and an argument of its own, and that refutation is only part of the exercise.

Develop your own positive theory of the case. Underlying your refutation is the premise that your case is superior to your opponent's. Almost all refutation therefore involves not only destroying your opponent's view of the case but also substituting your own theme or version. Exceptions are limited but do exist. For example, if you are arguing that your opponent has failed to satisfy a burden of proof, you may not find it necessary to present a counterpoint.

On the other hand, developing a positive theory may be helpful in persuading the decision-maker that the burden has not been met. In a case where contributory negligence bars recovery, a plaintiff may want to emphasize the defendant's own negligence as she argues that she was not contributorily negligent. The theory here is that the stronger your argument regarding the defendant's negligence, the less likely the decision-maker will find the plaintiff's negligence contributed to the event.

Determine Whether Your Opponent Is Wrong about the Facts

Refute errors directly. Once you have blocked out your opponent's argument and studied its key parts, consider whether your opponent's factual underpinnings are true or contrary to the evidence. If your opponent's argument plays fast and loose with documents or testimony at key points, prepare to demonstrate this to your listener. Use a direct and forceful approach: "Don Smith never testified that the light was green. Let us review what Don Smith actually said."

Use demonstrative aids. Employ computer technology to show copies of documents in question or correct testimony. [*See* Secret 7, Use the Best Medium for the Message.] If appropriate, use playbacks of videotaped testimony to underscore your point about misstatements of facts. There is nothing more devastating than clear contradiction of falsity. Look for it and point it out. If your opponent in closing argument states that Mrs. Waters clearly identified the defendant as the person who committed the crime, show to the jury the tape in which she stated she was not sure about her identification.

Refute only significant facts. Do not select insignificant factual errors for attack. Doing so may annoy your listener, making her feel that you are wasting time on matters of no importance.

Challenge Your Opponent's Evidence

Show the witness's bias. Showing bias is an effective way to challenge the credibility of a witness's testimony, for example, revealing that an alibi witness is the defendant's mother or spouse or that the government's witness is testifying as the result of a plea bargain.[2]

Argue That Testimony Is Unreliable

You can attack your opponent's evidence by arguing that a particular witness was not in a position to know what he testified to knowing. This is similar to attacking a witness's credibility on cross-examination. For example, you might argue that a witness did not actually observe the collision at issue but only heard it. Perhaps a medical expert witness did not actually treat or examine the plaintiff. If a witness was confused or upset or demonstrated a poor memory, point this out in your refutation. Perhaps a witness made inconsistent statements and should not be believed. Raise issues regarding the witness's reputation for truthfulness, his conviction of a crime, or prior unsavory conduct. An expert witness may lack credentials or qualifications or did not make a careful and full investigation of the facts.[3]

Argue that testimony is improbable. Demonstrating that your opponent's version of the case is improbable can be an effective way to refute the opposing argument. In England's famous Queen Caroline case in 1820 in which the king charged the queen with adultery, Henry Brougham, arguing for the queen, obtained in answer to most of his questions to Theodore Majocchi, the King's leading witness, the answer "no mi ricordo" ("I do not remember"). Brougham successfully argued that Majocchi could not possibly fail to remember so many facts relating to things an eyewitness would surely recall.[4]

Point out irrelevancies. Frequently, you can argue that the evidence presented by your opponent is irrelevant or otherwise useless in terms of resolving the case. Perhaps a learned treatise relied upon by your opponent is out of date, or a fact emphasized by your opponent is irrelevant in terms of causation. For example, the fact that a plaintiff did not fasten his seat belt until twenty minutes after he started driving has no bearing on the failure of the seatbelt to work at the time of the collision, three hours later.

Point out where significant evidence has been ignored. During argument in a civil case for assault, your opponent argues that the plaintiff was the first aggressor. However, she does not call attention to the fact that before arriving at the scene, the defendant went home and searched for an old hunting knife that he brought with him to the scene. Clearly, you would argue that your opponent ignored the very conduct that shows the defendant's intent.

Point out evidence given undue weight. Another effective means of refutation is to point out that your opponent is emphasizing evidence out of proportion to its importance. If the plaintiff's counsel in a medical malpractice case dwells on the defendant's alleged misdiagnosis of the decedent, you might point out that the evidence is overwhelming that even if the decedent was initially misdiagnosed, she would have died anyway.

Point Out Logical Fallacies

Analyze your opponent's argument logically. As discussed in an earlier chapter, logical fallacies can prove fatal to an argument. [*See* Secret 4, Base Your Argument on Reasons.] Analyze the structure of your opponent's argument. Does it hang together? Does it make sense?

Indirectly Argue That Testimony Is Improbable

Chicago lawyer Weymouth Kirkland was called upon to defend an insurance company in a case where the plaintiff claimed entitlement to funds based on the death of a policyholder. The defense asserted that the policyholder did not fall from a ship and drown, as alleged, instead contending that he walked off the ship very much alive.[5] A key witness for the plaintiff was the ship's cook. The following is from Kirkland's cross-examination of the cook at trial:

Q. How long had you known Peck (the policyholder)?
A. Fifteen years.
Q. You knew him well?
A. Yes, sir.
Q. How did you happen to see his body?
A. I looked out of the porthole.
Q. You recognized it beyond doubt as the body of Peck?
A. Yes, sir.
Q. Did you make any outcry when you saw the body?
A. No, sir.
Q. Did you ask the captain to stop the ship?
A. No, sir.
Q. What were you doing when you happened to look out of the window and saw the body?
A. I was peeling potatoes.

Q. And when the body of your old friend, Peck, floated by, you just kept on peeling potatoes?
A. Yes, sir.

During closing argument, Kirkland did not argue to the jury that the cook's testimony was false. Instead, he took a potato and knife from his pocket (you could bring knives into the courtroom in those days), rested his foot on a chair, and began to peel the potato. As he did this, he said to the jury, "What ho! What have we here? Who is this floating past? As I live and breathe, if it isn't my old friend Peck! I shall tell the captain about this in the morning. In the meantime, I must go right on peeling my potatoes." The jury came to its own conclusions.

Focus on precisely where the flaws are. Perhaps the problem is simple illogic, and your opponent has asserted a conclusion that has no connection with the factual premise. For example, opposing counsel argues: "After the new testing device was administered to the patient, she suffered a coronary. Thus, the device was defective." You would refute this argument by pointing out that one cannot infer causation merely because one event chronologically followed another.

Look for broad generalities. Another logical flaw in an argument may appear as a generalization from evidence of a single instance to a broad conclusion. More data may be needed to ensure that the conclusion is sound. If your opponent argues that her client's lost profits are based on the two preceding years, you might point out that using only two years of prior history is insufficient to predict future lost profits. In the same way, evidence about a characteristic of a large group of people does not always lead to a sound conclusion that the characteristic is true of a single member of the group. [*See* Secret 4, Base Your Argument on Reasons.]

Identify distortions and distractions. Consider whether the other side's argument depends on distortions and distractions—arguments that have nothing to do with what is really at stake. Your opponent's argument may have set up a straw man—an artificial claim that is not your position but that has the virtue (for the other side) of being rebuttable. Your opponent may have abandoned logic altogether and founded her argument on an appeal to emotion, tradition, sympathy, or even worse, prejudice or bias. If so, your refutation should point this out.

Argue That Your Opponent's Argument Is Contrary to the Law

This basic principle, although obvious, takes on interesting permutations when both sides argue that the law supports their position. It will usually be your analysis of case law or statutory construction that is required to persuade the decision-maker that the law supports your point of view rather than your opponent's. [*See* Secret 5, Build with Law, Evidence, and Policy.]

Argue That Your Opponent's Argument Contravenes Public Policy

There is an old story of a young lawyer who asked his mentor what to do in arguing a case if the facts were against him. The mentor advised him, "Argue the law." The student then asked what to do if the law were against him, and the reply was, "Argue the facts." The young lawyer then asked, "What if both the law and facts are against us?" "Then argue public policy" was the mentor's advice. Public policy considerations can provide compelling reasons to decide a conflict in a particular way. Courts regularly base their decisions on public policy, and you should always take advantage of opportunities to advance your position based on such considerations.

Counter Emotional Themes

Substitute an emotional appeal with a theme of your own. Although dealing appropriately with appeals to emotion in refutation can sometimes be difficult, it is essential to do so because emotional appeals can be very effective. [*See* Secret 6, Appeal to Emotion.] Jurors reduced to tears by the plight of an employee wrongfully terminated from her job will not be in an ideal mood to listen to you explain how the plaintiff failed to comply with several paragraphs of her contract. Rather than arguing "The other side does not want you to think; it wants you to ignore the facts and decide based entirely on what you feel," you must find a way to change the mood of the jury and lead them along a different path. In a case where the plaintiff is arguing wrongful discharge based on sexual harassment and has created an emotional appeal, you might argue:

"Although sexual harassment has no place in corporate America, asserting the false claim of sexual harassment is just as wrong."

Develop an Effective Format to Convey Your Refutation

Organize your refutation. Once you have identified the points to refute in your opponent's argument, you must decide on an effective order or arrangement for your refutation. This exercise involves the same kind of analysis you use in preparing your own argument. [*See* Secret 8, Strategically Arrange Your Arguments.]

Break Your Opponent's Emotional Hold on Your Listener

Breaking the "spell" created by your opponent's appeal to emotion is often one of the great challenges of refutation. If your opponent has created a sympathetic atmosphere for her position, break the emotional spell by refocusing your listener and changing the mood. Some advocates have been known to begin their arguments for the defense with a variation of the following: "Good morning, members of the jury. If I hold my hand before you and ask whether you see it, most of you would probably say 'yes'. But you really do not see my hand. What you see is only the front of my hand. You do not see my entire hand until I turn it around. Such is this case: You do not see the entire case until after the defense has had its chance to present evidence. Now let me tell you what this case is really about."[6]

Establish a format. One effective approach includes the following steps:

1. Identify the points you intend to refute.
2. Present your refuting points.
3. Develop support for your refutation.
4. Demonstrate the significance of your refutation.

The following is an example of using this four-part format for an oral argument in appellate court:

Step 1: Identify your point. "Your Honor, Mrs. Jones has suggested that the *Lusby* case abolished inter-spousal immunity and that, therefore, public policy cannot bar this case for fraud and intentional infliction of emotional distress."

Step 2: State your position. "The *Lusby* case does not eviscerate inter-spousal immunity in every case."

Step 3: Provide your support. "The Court of Appeals abolished inter-spousal immunity only in the limited situation in which a husband physically brutalized his wife. The court in *Lusby* was clear that public policy should always be considered in cases where one spouse sues another. Consider what the court wrote in its opinion:

> *We hold that in this unique situation, inter-spousal immunity cannot prevent the wife from suing her husband. Nevertheless, we must examine each situation separately when a spouse sues his or her spouse to determine if public policy permits the claim."*

Step 4: State the impact on the case. "Your Honor, the facts of this case are such that, under applicable case law, public policy does bar the claim. The *Lusby* case does not abolish public policy as a defense to all inter-spousal suits."

Make the Most of Having the Last Word

The opportunity for rebuttal is usually provided to the party having the burden of proof. Since the one who has the burden of proof is deemed to have the more difficult task of persuading, law and policy afford that party the opportunity for rebuttal, or the final opportunity to persuade. Always make the most of that opportunity.

Take cues from your listener. As stressed in previous chapters, watching and listening to questions asked by your listener contribute to a winning argument. Watching and listening will help you select the points to rebut. You may observe the listener's intense interest at a particular point of your opponent's presentation, which might signal that you must undermine that point on rebuttal. [*See* Secret 2, Tailor Your Argument to the Decision-Maker.]

Deliver a strong conclusion in your refutation. As we discussed in an earlier chapter, the conclusion can serve many purposes. [*See* Secret 8, Strategically Arrange Your Arguments.] When you are in rebuttal, you have the last word. Your conclusion can be the driving force of winning. Here is the opportunity to inspire your listener, to underscore the important points you advanced earlier, to summarize your position, and to involve your listener's emotion.

NOTES

1. Russell R. Windes and Arthur Hastings, *Argumentation and Advocacy* p. 193 (1966, Random House).

2. For an excellent discussion of attacking a witness for bias, see Steven Lubet, *Modern Trial Advocacy* (3d ed.) (2004, National Institute for Trial Advocacy).

3. For an excellent discussion of attacking a witness's credibility, see Thomas A. Mauet, *Trial Techniques* (6th ed.) (2002, Little, Brown and Company).

4. John Lord Campbell, *Lives of the Lord Chancellors and Keepers of the Great Seal of England* Vol. 8 p. 313 (1973, AMS Press, Inc.).

5. Lloyd Paul Stryker, *The Art of Advocacy* pp. 126–127 (1979, Zenger Publishing Company).

6. *See* Michael E. Tigar, *Persuasion: The Litigator's Art* p. 79 (1998, American Bar Association, Litigation Section). *Compare* Herbert J. Stern, *Trying Cases to Win* p. 210 (1991, Wiley and Sons); *see also* James W. McElhaney, *McElhaney's Trial Notebook* (3d ed.) "Breaking the Spell" p. 114 (1994, American Bar Association, Litigation Section).

Index

F

P

Q

About the Authors

Ronald J. Waicukauski is a trial lawyer with the Indianapolis law firm of Price, Waicukauski & Riley, LLC. For many years, he has been recognized in *Best Lawyers in America* and *Indiana Super Lawyers*. His areas of practice are diverse, covering a wide variety of matters in business, tort, and class-action litigation. He formerly served as a JAG in the U.S. Marine Corps and as the elected prosecuting attorney in Monroe County, Indiana.

Mr. Waicukauski received his undergraduate degree in speech, with distinction, from Northwestern University, his J.D. degree from Harvard University, where he was named Best Oralist in the Ames Competition, and his LL.M. degree, with Highest Honors, from George Washington University in 1976. He has taught trial and appellate advocacy at the Indiana University Schools of Law in Bloomington and Indianapolis, and as a faculty member of the National Institute of Trial Advocacy and the Defense Counsel Trial Academy. Mr. Waicukauski has also served as President, Indianapolis American Inn of Court, and as co-chair, Training the Advocate Committee, Litigation Section, American Bar Association.

Mr. Waicukauski is the author, co-author, or contributing author of numerous publications, including: *Learning the Craft*, Litigation (Spring 1998); *Ethos and the Art of Argument*, Litigation (Fall 1999); *The Winning Argument* (ABA 2001); *Defense Counsel Training Manual* (IADC 1995); *Quality Practice Management: A Manual for Law Firms* (IADC 1995);

and *Law and Amateur Sports* (Ind. Univ. Press 1982). He has been a frequent CLE speaker at meetings of the American Bar Association, the Indiana State Bar Association, and for many legal organizations in other states.

Paul Mark Sandler is a trial lawyer with a national reputation for successfully representing notable clients in trial and appellate courts. He is a partner in the Baltimore law firm of Shapiro Sher Guinot & Sandler, P.A., and is known for his thorough representation of clients, as evidenced by his remarkable courtroom victories.

Mr. Sandler is the author of *Anatomy of a Trial: A Primer for Young Lawyers*; *Raising the Bar: Practice Tips and Trial Techniques for Young Maryland Lawyers*; co-author of *Pleading Causes of Action in Maryland*; *Model Witness Examinations*; *The Winning Argument*; *Discovery Problems and Their Solutions*; *Maryland Discovery Problems and Solutions*, and *Pattern Examinations of Witnesses for the Maryland Lawyer*, and co-editor of *Appellate Practice for the Maryland Lawyer: State and Federal*. He is a frequent columnist for *The Daily Record*, is a lecturer and speaker throughout the United States, and is a member of the Union of International Advocates. He received his undergraduate degree from Hobart College, his law degree from Georgetown University Law Center, and was admitted to the Maryland Bar in 1972. Mr. Sandler is the founder and former Chair of the Litigation Section of the Maryland State Bar Association, and is the immediate past Secretary of the Litigation Section of the American Bar Association.

JoAnne A. Epps is the Dean and Professor of Law at Temple University's Beasley School of Law. She has been a member of the Temple Law faculty since 1985 and served as Associate Dean for

Academic Affairs from 1989–2008. Her primary teaching areas include criminal procedure, evidence, and trial advocacy.

Dean Epps is the co-author of *100 Vignettes for Improving Trial Evidence: Making & Meeting Objections*; *The Winning Argument*; and *Trial Evidence: Making and Meeting Objections* (2nd edition). She has also authored or co-authored several articles and book chapters. Dean Epps is a frequent lecturer and speaker on evidence and advocacy, both domestically and internationally, as well as a long-time faculty member of the National Institute of Trial Advocacy. Prior to joining the Temple Law faculty she was a deputy city attorney for the City of Los Angeles from 1976–1980 and an Assistant U.S. Attorney for the Eastern District of Pennsylvania from 1980–1985. Dean Epps is a member of the American Law Institute and an officer of the American Bar Association Section of Litigation. She received her B.A. degree from Trinity College in Hartford, Connecticut, in 1973 and her J.D. degree from Yale Law School in 1976.